NIETZSCHE'S
ON THE GENEALOGY OF MORALS

Continuum *Reader's Guides*

Continuum's *Reader's Guides* are clear, concise and accessible introductions to classic works of philosophy. Each book explores the major themes, historical and philosophical context and key passages of a major philosophical text, guiding the reader toward a thorough understanding of often demanding material. Ideal for undergraduate students, the guides provide an essential resource for anyone who needs to get to grips with a philosophical text.

***Reader's Guides* available from Continuum:**

NIETZSCHE'S
ON THE GENEALOGY OF
MORALS
A Reader's Guide

DANIEL CONWAY

continuum

Continuum International Publishing Group
The Tower Building   80 Maiden Lane
11 York Road   Suite 704
London SE1 7NX   New York, NY 10038

www.continuumbooks.com

First published 2008

British Library Cataloguing-in-Publication Data
A catalogue record for this book is available from the British Library.

ISBN-10: 0-8264-7816-6 (hardback)
          0-8264-7817-4 (paperback)
ISBN-13: 978-0-8264-7816-0 (hardback)
          978-0-8264-7817-7 (paperback)

Library of Congress Cataloging-in-Publication Data
A catalog record of this book is available from the Library of Congress.

Typeset by Servis Filmsetting Ltd, Manchester
Printed and bound in Great Britain by
MPG Books Ltd, Bodmin, Cornwall

CONTENTS

ACKNOWLEDGEMENTS

I am pleased to acknowledge the hospitality of the administration and staff of the National Humanities Center, where I was a visiting Fellow in 2006–07. I also wish to recognize the generosity of the Delta Delta Delta sorority, which endowed the Fellowship I was awarded. My residence at the Center was made possible by a generous research leave granted by The College of Liberal Arts at Texas A&M University.

I also wish to express my gratitude to the many friends and colleagues who have shared with me their passion for Nietzsche's philosophy. For this project, I am particularly indebted to Christa Davis Acampora, Ralph Acampora, Roberto Alejandro, Keith Ansell-Pearson, Babette Babich, Robert Gooding-Williams, Lawrence Hatab, Paul Loeb, Robert Pippin, Aaron Ridley, Alan Schrift, John Seery, T. K. Seung, Gary Shapiro, Herman Siemens, Tracy Strong and John Wilcox. I owe a special debt of gratitude to David Owen, who not only commented on an early draft of the manuscript, but also allowed me to read his own manuscript, which has since been published. Claire Katz, to whom I already owe everything, also provided instructive commentary on early drafts of the manuscript. Finally, I would like to thank Olivia and Evelyn Conway, who remind me each day of the wonders of genealogy and the dangers of morality.

I have recycled a few sentences from each of the following essays: '*Wir Erkennenden*: Self-referentiality in *Zur Genealogie der Moral*', *Journal of Nietzsche Studies*, Issue 22, Fall 2001, pp. 116–32. 'How We Became What We Are: Tracking The "Beasts of Prey"', in *Nietzsche's*

ACKNOWLEDGEMENTS

On the Genealogy of Morals: *Critical Essays*, ed. Christa Davis Acampora. Lanham, MD: Rowman & Littlefield, 2006, pp. 305–20.

College Station, Texas
September 2007

A NOTE ON TRANSLATIONS

Throughout this *Reader's Guide*, I have relied primarily on Walter Kaufmann's translation of *Zur Genealogie der Moral*, which he prepared in collaboration with R. J. Hollingdale for Random House. On several occasions I have altered the text of the Kaufmann and Hollingdale translation to accommodate improvements suggested by other, more recent translations. (Full citations for these translations are found in the Bibliography.) Finally, on several occasions I have altered the text of the Kaufmann and Hollingdale translation in favour of my own translations, especially in order to correct for formulations that are now dated, anachronistic, non-standard or misleadingly non-neutral in gender specification. In making these alterations, I have relied on the text of *Zur Genealogie der Moral* that appears in Volume 5 of *Friedrich Nietzsche, Sämtliche Werke: Kritische Studienausgabe in 15 Bänden* (KSA), eds G. Colli and M. Montinari. Berlin: dtv/de Gruyter, 1980.

ABBREVIATIONS

The following key explains the abbreviations I have used to identify citations from Nietzsche's writings. Lower-case instances of these abbreviations are meant to identify citations from Nietzsche's review of his books in *Ecce Homo*. (Citations from other chapters of *Ecce Homo* are designated by 'wise', 'clever', 'books' and 'destiny'.) Citations drawn from Nietzsche's various Prefaces and Epigraphs are designated by P and E, respectively. In all instances, numbers refer to sections rather than to pages. In the long chapter devoted to 'Reading the Text', no references are provided for citations extracted from the particular section under consideration.

A: *The Antichrist*, in *The Portable Nietzsche*, ed. and trans. Walter Kaufmann. New York: Viking Penguin, 1982.

BGE: *Beyond Good and Evil: Prelude to a Philosophy of the Future*, trans. Walter Kaufmann. New York: Random House/Vintage Books, 1989.

BT: *The Birth of Tragedy,* trans. Walter Kaufmann (compiled with *The Case of Wagner*, trans. Walter Kaufmann). New York: Random House/Vintage Books, 1967.

D: *Daybreak* [also, *The Dawn*]*: Thoughts on the Prejudices of Morality*, trans. R. J. Hollingdale. Cambridge: Cambridge University Press, 1982.

EH: *Ecce Homo*, trans. Walter Kaufmann (compiled with *On the Genealogy of Morals*, trans. Walter Kaufmann and R. J. Hollingdale). New York: Random House/Vintage Books, 1989.

GM: *On the Genealogy of Morals*, trans. Walter Kaufmann and R. J. Hollingdale (compiled with *Ecce Homo*, trans.

	Walter Kaufmann). New York: Random House/Vintage Books, 1989.
GS:	*The Gay Science*, trans. Walter Kaufmann. New York: Random House/Vintage Books, 1974.
HH:	*Human, All-Too-Human: A Book for Free Spirits*, trans. R. J. Hollingdale. Cambridge: Cambridge University Press, 1986.
SB:	*Sämtliche Briefe: Kritische Studienausgabe in 8 Bänden*, ed. G. Colli and M. Montinari. Berlin: dtv/de Gruyter, 1986.
TI:	*Twilight of the Idols*, in *The Portable Nietzsche*, ed. and trans. Walter Kaufmann. New York: Viking Penguin, 1982.
WP:	*The Will to Power*, trans. Walter Kaufmann and R. J. Hollingdale, ed. Walter Kaufmann. New York: Random House/Vintage Books, 1968.
Z:	*Thus Spoke Zarathustra*, in *The Portable Nietzsche*, ed. and trans. Walter Kaufmann. New York: Viking Penguin, 1982.

CHAPTER 1

CONTEXT

Friedrich Wilhelm Nietzsche was born on 15 October 1844 in the village of Röcken, in Prussian Saxony. The son and grandson of Lutheran pastors, he spent his early years in and around the local parsonage. When his father died in 1849, his mother moved the family to the nearby town of Naumburg, where young Fritz attended the local Gymnasium. He was later selected for admission to the prestigious boarding school in Pforta, where he received a traditional education in classical studies. At Bonn University, he studied theology and philosophy before transferring to Leipzig University, where he studied classical philology under the direction of Friedrich Ritschl (1806–76), whom he had also known at Bonn. On the strength of Ritschl's recommendation, Nietzsche was appointed in 1869 to the Chair in Classical Philology at the University of Basel (in Switzerland), even though he had not yet completed the requirements for his doctoral degree.

Nietzsche's tenure at Basel was interrupted by military service (as a medical orderly in the Franco–Prussian War), recurring bouts of illness, and a growing sense of dissatisfaction with the field of academic philology. While posted at Basel, he nevertheless completed and published a number of books and essays, including *The Birth of Tragedy from the Spirit of Music* (1872), the four *Untimely Meditations* (1873–6), and *Human, All-Too-Human* (1878). Citing poor health, he resigned his university appointment in 1879.

Nietzsche spent the remainder of his sane life writing books and leading a nomadic existence. In constant pursuit of a more suitable climate for his work, he shuttled regularly between the Upper Engadine region in Switzerland and various destinations in Italy, including Venice, Nice and Turin. In this prolific post-academic period, he wrote *The Wanderer and His Shadow* (1880), *The Dawn* (1881), *The Gay Science* (1882), *Thus Spoke Zarathustra* (1883–5), *Beyond Good and Evil* (1886), *On the Genealogy of Morals* (1887), and a number of new prefaces, appendices, poems and other materials. In 1888, his final year of sanity, he wrote *The Case of Wagner, Twilight of the Idols* (published in 1889), *The Antichrist* and *Nietzsche contra Wagner* (published in 1895) and *Ecce Homo* (published in 1908).

In January of 1889, Nietzsche's philosophical career came to an end. As legend has it, he collapsed into madness while protecting a carriage horse from the cruel blows of its driver.[1] After a brief period of hospitalization, followed by a year-long institutionalization in Jena, he returned with his mother to her Naumburg home, where he led a mostly peaceful existence. He received occasional visitors, took long walks, and improvised at the piano for hours on end.[2] In 1893, Nietzsche and his mother were joined in Naumburg by his sister, Elisabeth Förster-Nietzsche, who had returned to Germany following the suicide of her husband and the failure of their colonial adventure in Paraguay. Intending to capitalize on her brother's growing fame, Elisabeth fostered a cult-like enthusiasm for his books and teachings, oversaw the founding of the Nietzsche Archive, and produced a two-volume biography of her brother. When their mother died in 1897, Elisabeth moved her brother and the Archive to Weimar. Friedrich Nietzsche finally died on 25 August 1900.

On the Genealogy of Morals (hereafter, GM) was composed in the summer of 1887 and published in November of that year. As had increasingly become his practice, Nietzsche worked quickly and efficiently, finishing the whole of GM in approximately four weeks of concentrated effort.[3] His writing was facilitated by the continuity of the themes addressed in GM with those treated in other writings from the post-Zarathustran period of his career, including *Beyond Good and Evil*,[4] which he published in 1886; the retrospective prefaces he added in 1886 to the new editions of *The Birth of Tragedy, Human, All-Too-Human* (Parts I and II), *The Dawn* and *The Gay Science*; and Book V of *The Gay Science*, which he composed in October of 1886. This is not to suggest, however, that GM is devoid of novelty. While there is much in GM that is either ancillary or derivative, the book is rightly praised for the originality of the insights it conveys.

As Nietzsche himself confirms, GM is also indebted to the books that preceded it for the refinement of its unique approach to the history of morality. He identifies GM as the culmination of a series of inquiries that commenced with the publication of *Human, All-Too-Human* in 1878. As he tells the story, which is essentially a genealogy of GM, these predecessor inquiries afforded him the opportunity to rehearse and clarify his 'thoughts on the *origin* of our moral prejudices' (GM P2). That the practice of contemporary morality trades on a cluster of unacknowledged prejudices is in fact a central theme of this series of inquiries. In GM itself, as we shall see, he wishes to demonstrate that these prejudices endow contemporary morality with a past that is far more complicated, far more burdensome, and far more interesting, than rival scholars have dared to suppose. Indeed, his use of the word *prejudice* in this context is meant to convey his belief, which GM is meant to corroborate, that the actual worth of our highest values remains as yet unknown to us.

Nietzsche is especially keen to distinguish *his* approach to the history of morality from the approach favoured by the 'English psychologists' (GM I: 1). Although he names only Paul Rée (who was not English, but German), this group is apparently meant to include such figures as Francis Hutcheson (1694–1746), David Hume (1711–76), Jeremy Bentham (1748–1832), and John Stuart Mill (1806–73).[5] While grateful to these predecessors for their groundbreaking research, as well as for their abstention from supernatural principles of explanation, he nevertheless faults them for uncritically assuming the primacy and constancy of their own values. As a result of their failure to discern the historical *development* of moral values, their potentially fruitful inquiries into the history of morality invariably devolve into perfunctory exercises confirming the constancy of 'English' customs and manners.

Like his rivals among the English psychologists, Nietzsche resolves to explain the origin of moral values without recourse to supernatural principles of explanation. Just one year earlier, in *Beyond Good and Evil* (which GM is meant to 'supplement and clarify'), he conducted a similar investigation under the heading 'Toward a Natural History of Morals' [*Zur Naturgeschichte der Moral*]. At the same time, however, his alternative approach to the history of morality is meant to furnish the 'historical spirit' that is lacking in his predecessors and rivals. This means, as we shall see, that Nietzsche offers to determine the *genuine* origins of our most cherished moral values, even if doing so obliges him to place these values in an unfamiliar, unflattering light.

It is for this reason, in fact, that he develops his alternative approach under the rubric of *genealogy*. In contrast to his predecessors and rivals, he intends to document those familial relationships and resemblances – heretofore unnoticed or unreported – that suggest a connection between seemingly antithetical values and value systems. Just as any conventional genealogy is bound to disclose the wayward ramifications of an otherwise majestic family tree, so a genealogy of morals is likely to reveal the uninspiring, plebeian origins of regnant values. The 'selfless' values that we now honour, he thus insists, are in fact descended from a resentment-fuelled slave morality, while the 'selfish' values that we now shun were at one time ingredient to the *ethos* of a dominant noble morality.

To be sure, the very notion of a *genealogy* of morals may strike us as odd. Genealogy, after all, is the science or study of kinship relations and familial descent. It is most commonly practised to determine the pedigree of domestic livestock, to map the kinship structure of 'primitive' tribes and peoples, to chart lines of hereditary succession, and to unearth the ancestral roots of individuals and families in search of a stable sense of identity. Genealogical terms and images are also used, albeit more figuratively, to establish the transmission of ideas and cultural artefacts, to describe the propagation of schools of thought, and to measure the historical influence of writers, thinkers and artists.

What Nietzsche finds most appealing about the science of genealogy is its appreciation of the present as always already encumbered by the claims of the past. The goal of any genealogy is to situate individuals within the larger context of the families from which they are descended. These families are in turn placed within the extended kinship networks to which they belong. As these larger networks are disclosed, individuals are likely to discover that certain opportunities have been opened (or closed) to them simply by virtue of the particular families and kinship networks to which they belong. Pretenders to a throne may discover that they belong to the right (or wrong) lineage, while claimants to a legacy may find themselves qualified (or disqualified) for reasons beyond their control. Genetic testing may reveal that certain individuals are advantaged (or disadvantaged) simply by virtue of the accident of their ancestry.

As a genealogist of morals, Nietzsche is concerned to reveal the various ways in which the contemporary practice of morality is shaped by its past. Although he furnishes his readers with no orienting definition of the term *morality*,[6] he occasionally draws their attention to what he considers to be the most salient characteristics of morality. In his Preface, for example, he singles out the positive value assigned to the 'instincts of pity, self-abnegation, [and] self-sacrifice' (GM P5). In Essay I, he associates morality with the creative expression of *ressentiment*, to which he attributes the origin of the familiar opposition between *good* and *evil*. In Essay II, he exposes the practice of morality as dangerously reliant on the motivation furnished by an ever-escalating feeling of guilt. In Essay III, he reveals morality to be dependent on the ascetic ideal, which honours the life of self-deprivation as the highest standard of human flourishing.[7] Finally, at the close of GM, he exposes the *will to nothingness* that morality both presupposes and expresses. As this progression suggests, the complex character of morality is meant to emerge gradually over the course of GM, as Nietzsche challenges his readers to experience for themselves the previously unknown and unimaginable truth of morality.

He thus aims in GM to introduce us to morality as a shared cultural inheritance, which claims and shapes us prior to any judgements we might form about it. Just as conventional genealogies disclose that which we can neither choose nor change about ourselves – namely the identity and dominant attributes of our ancestors – so Nietzsche's genealogy of morals is meant to reveal the extent to which we are antecedently formed by our shared cultural inheritance. He is particularly concerned in GM to disclose the complex and diverse ways in which morality has become constitutive of our identity, such that we simply take for granted its superlative value.

We should not conclude, however, that Nietzsche's sole concern in GM is simply to acquaint us with the unquestioned, and heretofore unquestionable, role that morality plays in our lives. He also hopes to persuade us of the potentially *deadly* burden of our shared cultural inheritance, such that our continued participation in the practice of morality threatens to bleed human existence of all remaining meaning, purpose and hope. Morality has encouraged us to become ever more fully civilized, thereby securing the conditions of our continued survival, but it has done so by placing the very future of humankind in doubt.

Nietzsche advertises GM as a *polemic*,[8] by which he means to convey three related points. First of all, he intends to pick a fight with contemporary morality and its champions. The case he builds against morality is meant to be provocative, aggressive, persistent, unsentimental, compelling and, most importantly, victorious. As a polemic, that is, GM presents the kind of case against morality that is meant to benefit from the energy and affect expended in its service. Nietzsche thus indulges himself in rhetorical excesses that are not typically associated with the sober practice of scholarly research. While this does not mean that he is indifferent to the plausibility and truth of the hypotheses he advances in GM,[9] it *does* mean that he will do what is needed to provoke the desired response in his target audience.[10] If necessary, as we shall see, he will pander to the growing (if naive) secularism of his readers, play upon their quasi-religious fears of apocalypse, exploit their unearned vanity and capitalize on the nervous uncertainty that their optimism so cleverly masks.

Second, the case he builds against morality is deeply, unmistakably and unabashedly *personal*. He does not pretend to approach the problem of morality with anything like an open mind. Throughout GM, Nietzsche regularly draws our attention to his own stake in the investigation he conducts, occasionally intimating the hopes and fears that motivate his inquiry. He freely volunteers his 'fundamental mistrust' of the altruistic instincts he vows to investigate (GM P5), and he openly voices his suspicion that 'precisely morality was [and remains] the danger of dangers' (GM P6). While some readers will be put off by this aspect of Nietzsche's polemic, the readers whom he hopes to attract will be intrigued, perhaps even seduced, by the attention he draws to his personal stake in the agenda he pursues. If they are to join him in his quest, in fact, they too must acquire or develop a similarly personal stake in the timely destruction of Christian morality.

Third, his genealogy of morals is meant to mobilize his readers and call them to arms. In addition to its overtly retrospective focus, GM also displays an unmistakably prospective focus, as Nietzsche attempts to orient his readers to the question of the future of humankind. Like all practitioners of genealogy, that is, he turns to the past in order to support a particular interpretation of the present and a corresponding vision of the future. The main narrative of GM is meant not only to explain the genesis of our current predicament, but also to establish the possibility of our transition to an extramoral future. If he tells this story effectively, or so he believes, his readers will be changed in their reception of it, perhaps to the extent that they will join him in his self-consuming assault on Christian morality.

They are likely to do so, however, only in the event that he persuades them of the urgency of their participation in his war on Christian morality. While any number of readers might support a campaign to eradicate the influence and practice of Christian morality, GM specifically targets those readers who understand that the final, decisive assault on morality must be *self*-directed. That is, GM is meant to recruit and train readers who are prepared to turn their critical energies against the residuum of Christian morality – in the form of the will to truth – that lingers *within them*. By hosting the final act in the self-destruction of Christian morality, Nietzsche and his 'we' will contribute, or so he anticipates, to the production of an extra-moral future. They will be changed, perhaps even destroyed, in the process, but Christian morality will be no more.

In light of what Nietzsche expects of his best readers, we should not be surprised to learn that the dramatic-rhetorical structure of GM is meant to facilitate their education and maturation. The three essays of GM are fashioned as training exercises, wherein Nietzsche regularly addresses his readers as he attempts to promote (and chart) their progress. Hoping to open their eyes (and other senses) without prematurely arresting their development, he gradually introduces his readers to previously unknown truths and perspectives. Along the way, he flatters and goads them, puts them on notice, warns and cautions them, lifts and sinks their spirits, and withholds crucial details that he may or may not disclose later on. Exercising equal parts caution and indirection, he guides them toward a progressively more comprehensive reckoning of the claims of morality on their lives.

Nietzsche's programme of education in GM is meant to guide his best readers in their passage from innocence to experience. This is a path that he himself has travelled, or so he claims, which is why he presents himself as uniquely qualified to conduct his readers on the journey described in GM. A convalescent in his own right, he draws on his own experience to promote and accelerate the convalescence of his readers. Throughout GM, in fact, he periodically displays the excess strength, intellectual conscience and good cheer that are indicative of his recent return to health. If these gratuitous displays of health have the desired effect, his best readers will embrace the destiny they share with him. Together, as a 'we', they will host the self-destruction of Christian morality and thereby inaugurate the extra-moral period of human history.

CHAPTER 2

OVERVIEW OF THEMES

PREFACE

The Preface to GM is intended to introduce Nietzsche to his likely readers. To this end, he presents his credentials as a genealogist of morals and explains the genesis of his novel approach to the history of morality. In doing so, he also discredits the methods and conclusions of his predecessors and presumed rivals, all of whom have failed to conduct an adequately *historical* investigation into the history of morality.

Nietzsche's most important objective in the Preface to GM is to present himself as a reliable guide to the undiscovered country of morality. His account of his own development, which he elsewhere describes as a process of *convalescence*, is meant to illuminate the path along which he now offers to conduct his best readers. Just as he learned to *see* new vistas and to *hear* a previously inaudible demand, so his best readers may expect, under his tutelage, to sharpen their senses, refine their sensibilities, regain their strength, improve their overall health, pursue wisdom, and awaken to the task that awaits them. He speaks authoritatively in GM, that is, because he has already discovered for himself the truth he now wishes to share with his target audience. Inasmuch as the main narrative of GM describes the reader's passage from innocence to experience, the Preface to GM is meant to convince us that Nietzsche is a credible leader of the journey of self-discovery that is about to commence.

ESSAY I: 'GOOD AND EVIL', 'GOOD AND BAD'

Synopsis

Essay I of GM introduces Nietzsche's famous distinction between the *noble morality*, which is predicated on the difference between 'good and bad', and the *slave morality*, which trades on the opposition between 'good and evil'. The noble morality originates in a spontaneous affirmation of oneself (and everything pertaining or belonging to oneself) as *good*, and only then designates everyone and everything else as *bad*. By way of contrast, the slave morality always originates in a denunciation of one's oppressors as *evil*, and only then pronounces oneself *good* on the basis of the suffering one chooses, supposedly, to endure.

In support of this distinction, Nietzsche sets out in Essay I to explain three related processes that he regards as integral to the historical development of morality: 1) how the slave morality arose in response to a pre-existing noble morality; 2) how the slave morality eventually conquered the noble morality; and 3) how the slave morality gained ascendancy, under the banner of Christian morality, within the larger development of European civilization. The key to his explanation of these processes is his account of the *slave revolt in morality*, by means of which the slaves established an alternative morality in which unwarranted suffering was acknowledged as the most reliable index of goodness. On the strength of this revolt, the slaves were able to transform the suffering they endured at the hands of their oppressors into their crowning virtue; they thereby learned to derive enormous power from an initial position of powerlessness. Nietzsche thus concludes that the virtues associated with *altruism* and *selflessness* – which contemporary morality honours without question – emerged within the context of a slave morality, whose practitioners were materially excluded from cultivating the naturally more desirable 'virtues' *egoism* and *selfishness*.

In his review of GM, Nietzsche draws our attention to his mastery of the 'art of surprise' (EH: gm). Among the many surprises in store for the reader of Essay I is Nietzsche's reliance on a dynamic model of history, which allows him to present the ongoing development of Western civilization as an amoral, open-ended 'struggle' between two competing value-systems. His reliance on this model of history furthermore positions him to characterize the contemporary dominion of slavish values as merely one chapter in a very long tale of reversal and alternation. If Nietzsche's readers are to embrace this model of history, they must temper their hopes for a permanent victory on the part of either value-system. While they need not renounce their partisan allegiances – especially if they share his enthusiasm for the periodic resurgence of the active forces that he associated with 'Rome' – they must be careful not to lose sight of the amoral struggle in which these competing value-systems are joined.

Analysis of sections

Following the practice adopted by Nietzsche in his review of GM in *Ecce Homo*, I have divided each of the three essays into a *beginning*, which is '*calculated* to mislead'; a *middle*, wherein 'eventually a *tempo feroce* is attained in which everything rushes ahead in a tremendous tension'; and an *end*, in which 'a *new* truth becomes visible' (EH: gm).

Beginning (Sections 1–6)

The beginning of Essay I introduces Nietzsche's alternative derivation of the origin of moral value judgements. These sections suggest, misleadingly, that Essay I is meant simply to express Nietzsche's uncomplicated preference for all things noble.

Sections 1–3: Critical engagement with the 'English psychologists' and their ahistorical approach to the history of morality.

Sections 4–6: Presentation of etymological evidence in support of the 'rule of conceptual transformation', which governs the process through which pre-moral concepts and terms resolve themselves into moral concepts and terms.

Middle (Sections 7–15)

In the middle of Essay I, Nietzsche develops his account of the slave revolt in morality. A *tempo feroce* is attained as he relates the teachings of revenge promulgated by Tertullian and St Thomas Aquinas. These teachings demonstrate that Christianity was born *not* 'out of the "spirit"', but 'out of the spirit of *ressentiment*' (EH: gm).

Sections 7–9: Polemical introduction to the Jews and their inversion of noble values.

Sections 10–13: Account of the process through which agents of *ressentiment* create a new morality predicated on the supposed opposition between *good* and *evil*.

Section 12 is presented as an involuntary digression, in which Nietzsche expresses his concern that morality has diminished humankind to the point that the future of the species is now in question.

Sections 14–15: Disclosure of the teaching of revenge that secretly informs the cultivation and practice of Christian virtues.

End (Sections 16–17)

The end of Essay I delivers a '*new* truth' concerning the protracted struggle between 'Rome' and 'Judea'. These sections confirm that Nietzsche and his readers must reconcile their allegiance to 'Rome' with their commitment to a dynamic, amoral model of historical development.

Sections 16–17: Characterization of the protracted struggle between the value-systems represented, respectively, by 'good and bad' and 'good and evil'.

ESSAY II: 'GUILT', 'BAD CONSCIENCE' AND THE LIKE

Synopsis

In this ambitious essay, Nietzsche offers an alternative account of the origin and development of the concept of *responsibility*. The account he provides is broadly anthropological in scope, and it is meant to cleave as strictly as possible to naturalistic principles of explanation. Noting the similarity between the German words for *guilt* and *debt*, he traces the origin of the contemporary, moral concept of responsibility to the primitive, pre-moral concept of indebtedness. In essence, he wishes to claim, human beings were made responsible through a gruesome, extended – and ongoing – process of cultivation, which he likens to the *breeding* of a wild animal. Central to this account are his novel explanations of the origin of *conscience* (via the mandatory introjection of animal aggression) and the acquisition of *memory* (via painful techniques of enforced implantation).

The breeding of the human animal became both possible and desirable, he speculates, with the violent founding of the earliest forms of civil society. The peace and security of civil society were originally achieved (and are sustained to this day), he proposes, only on the condition that civilized human beings refrain – under the penalty of death or exile – from outward (i.e. other-directed) expressions of their native animal aggression. Rather than vent their instinct for cruelty against others, civilized human beings are expected to direct their aggression against themselves. So it was, Nietzsche believes, that human beings became creatures of *conscience*, involuntarily possessed of interiority and uniquely disposed to cultivate these habits of self-attention.

As the suffering associated with the inward discharge of aggression became too great to bear, however, some of these creatures of conscience began to question the very meaning of their existence. As they did so, the option of 'suicidal nihilism' became increasingly attractive to them. At the suggestion of the ascetic priest, these miserable creatures sought – and subsequently found – the cause of their suffering in their dereliction of various duties and obligations. Having learned to interpret the call of conscience as a reminder of their outstanding debts and neglected obligations, they contracted the species-preserving illness of the *bad conscience*, which obliged them to cultivate those habits of self-attention that would best ensure their survival.

By contracting the illness of the bad conscience, the human animal became responsible, but it also exposed itself to an even more devastating illness: *guilt*. Duly accustomed to regarding itself as indebted, the human animal became increasingly susceptible to the suggestion that their debts were in fact irremediable. To find oneself guilty, Nietzsche explains, is to hold oneself responsible not only for one's acquired obligations, but also for the flawed nature of one's very being, which Christian morality presents as irreparably faulted. Those who deem themselves guilty, he further explains, may expect to gain rapturous relief from their suffering, for the punishment befitting a guilty agent is in principle limitless. This carries an intensified sense of meaning as they endeavour to stifle the evil impulses that reside within themselves.

While generally appreciative of the role of the bad conscience in securing the future of humankind, Nietzsche is concerned that Christian guilt has burdened the human species with a sense of responsibility that is both unsustainable and counter-selective. Although nature has thus far bred the human animal for survival, Nietzsche fears that the levelling influence of Christian morality will mark the species for extinction.

Nietzsche's 'mastery' of the 'art of surprise' enables him to deliver several insights to good rhetorical effect. First of all, his readers learn that the human being is a kind of animal, and that this animal is far

older, and far more variously evolved, than most historians of morality were inclined at the time to suppose. Second, Nietzsche advertises
his account of evolution as the basis for his *hope* that the self-inflicted
suffering associated with the bad conscience may yet develop into the
triumphant, extra-moral self-affirmation that he briefly sketches
toward the end of Essay II. Third, his readers may be surprised to
learn that his account of evolution in turn rests on an alternative
theory of *life*, which he also unveils, albeit briefly, in Essay II. The
essence of life, he proposes, is not self-preservation, but *will to power*.
A living being seeks first and foremost to expend its accumulated
stores of strength, *even* at the risk of dying in the ensuing process of
self-overcoming. Finally, Nietzsche's readers will certainly be surprised to learn that he and they are not equal to the prescribed task
of turning the bad conscience against itself. A lesser task awaits them.

Analysis of sections
Beginning (Sections 1–15)
The beginning of Essay II explains how the development of the creditor–debtor relationship encouraged primitive human beings to
acquire a personal sense of responsibility. These sections suggest,
misleadingly, that what Nietzsche here calls *responsibility* has little
or nothing to do with moral responsibility as we know it.
Sections 1–3: Preliminary account of the origins of responsibility,
with particular emphasis on the need for primitive human beings to
acquire a memory for their promises.
Sections 4–7: Introduction of the creditor–debtor relationship;
explanation of its role in the development of a distinctly *legal* sense
of personal responsibility.
Section 7 is presented as a digression from the main narrative. Here
we learn that human beings were 'more cheerful' when the cruelty
visited upon them was overt and uncomplicated.
Sections 8–12: Explanation of the role of the creditor–debtor relationship in the development of the community's understanding of
its relationship to its members, especially as this development is
reflected in the self-cancellation of *justice*.
Sections 11 and 12 are presented as digressions from the main narrative. The former section repudiates the popular notion that any
appeal to justice invariably betrays an expression of *ressentiment*,
while the latter section demonstrates the need to separate the 'origin'
of punishment from its 'purpose'.

Sections 13–15: Expanded discussion of punishment, with particular emphasis on the difference between its *procedure*, which is 'enduring', and its *meaning*, which is 'fluid'.

Middle (Sections 16–23)

The middle of Essay II comprises Nietzsche's account of the transformation of the concept of *debt* into the concept of *guilt*. A *tempo feroce* is attained as he exposes the 'madness of will' that informs the Christian teaching of guilt.

Sections 16–18: Presentation of Nietzsche's alternative hypothesis concerning the origin of the *bad conscience*, with particular emphasis on the violent conditions under which the most primitive states were founded.

Sections 19–20: Explanation of the role of the creditor–debtor relationship in the development of a distinctly *religious* sense of personal responsibility.

Sections 21–23: Explanation of the role of the creditor–debtor relationship in the development of a distinctly *moral* sense of personal responsibility.

End (Sections 24–25)

The end of Essay II delivers a '*new*' truth' concerning the future of the bad conscience. Although it would be possible to turn the power of the bad conscience against itself, and thereby declare war on our anti-affective breeding, we are not strong enough to assume responsibility for this task.

Sections 24–25: Evaluation of our prospects for turning the bad conscience against itself; invocation of the redemptive hero who someday will liberate humankind from the curse of the ascetic ideal.

ESSAY III: WHAT IS THE MEANING OF ASCETIC IDEALS?

Synopsis

In the final essay of GM, Nietzsche sets out to explain what it means that ascetic ideals have exerted such a powerful influence on the development of Western civilization. What the preponderance of ascetic ideals does *not* mean, he insists, is that human beings are ascetic either by choice, nature or divine decree. What it does mean, he contends, is that no other ideals have presented themselves for adoption. The ascetic ideal thus owes its preponderance throughout the moral period of human development to the monopoly it has enjoyed in the business of granting meaning to suffering human beings.

If no alternative ideals have been made available for consideration, he surmises, then it must be the case that the ascetic ideal serves the larger interests of life itself. It does so, he explains, by furnishing the sickliest of human beings with the optimal conditions under which they might maximize their experience of vitality and power. By encouraging these sufferers to disparage the value of life, the ascetic ideal distracts them from their woes, rouses their wearied affects, confers meaning upon their suffering, and generally underwrites their mitigated affirmation of life. The ascetic ideal thus enables a sickly will to project itself into the future. Fortified by this artificial injection of vitality, the ascetic vows to live another day, if only so that he might escalate his attack on the value of life. It is against this backdrop that Nietzsche develops his physiologicalpsychological profile of the ascetic priest, who, he proposes, serves the interests of life by providing for the protection and mutual aid of the sickliest of human beings. At the same time, however, he demonstrates that the ascetic priest is not a physician and should not be mistaken for one.

Nietzsche's 'mastery' of the 'art of surprise' is on full display in Essay III. Here we learn that *science* is not the conqueror of the ascetic ideal, but its final refuge. With its authority in marked decline, the ascetic ideal now motivates only those quirky scholars who maintain their faith in the saving power of truth. This means, of course, that Nietzsche and his fellow 'knowers', who still have faith in truth, are the final champions of the ascetic ideal. They can become genuine opponents of the ascetic ideal, which Nietzsche challenges them to do, only by turning against the will to truth that resides within themselves. Hence the final surprise that awaits Nietzsche's readers in GM: Any meaningful assault on Christian morality must be both self-directed and self-consuming. If his readers wish to facilitate the self-destruction of Christian morality, that is, they must be prepared to host its final, fatal act of self-interrogation. If they do so, he reveals, they will have no choice but to unleash against themselves the will to nothingness that animates their will to truth. In the end, that is, GM is meant to recruit readers and 'friends' who will risk their lives to ensure the final collapse of Christian morality.

Analysis of sections

Beginning (Sections 1–10)

The beginning of Essay III provides Nietzsche's readers with a general introduction to ascetic ideals, and it takes up the question of the meaning of ascetic ideals in the specific cases pertaining, respectively, to artists and philosophers. These sections suggest, misleadingly, that Nietzsche intends to oppose the ascetic ideal and, perhaps, to provide an alternative ideal.

Section 1: Introduction to the general question of the meaning of ascetic ideals, including a preview of various answers to this question.

Sections 2–4: Explanation of what ascetic ideals mean for artists.

Sections 5–10: Explanation of what ascetic ideals mean for philosophers, with particular emphasis on the use of the ascetic ideal by 'maternal' philosophers.

Middle (Sections 11–22)

The middle of Essay III comprises Nietzsche's physiological-psychological profile of the ascetic priest. *A tempo feroce* is attained as Nietzsche reveals the psychological principles underlying the priest's reliance on his 'guilty' method for treating depression.

Sections 11–12: Introduction to Nietzsche's explanation of what ascetic ideals mean for the priest.

Section 12 is presented as a digression from the main narrative. Here Nietzsche identifies the failings of the familiar, ascetic approach to philosophy and warns his readers to beware of the 'conceptual fiction' on which it trades.

Sections 13–14: Physiological account of the ascetic ideal as an artifice in the service of life.

Sections 15–16: Physiological account of the ascetic priest as an agent in the service of life.

Sections 17–18: Critical evaluation of the priest's credentials as a physician, with particular emphasis on his 'innocent' methods for treating depression.

Sections 19–22: Critical evaluation of the priest's credentials as a physician, with particular emphasis on his 'guilty' method for treating depression.

End (Sections 23–28)

The end of Essay III delivers a *'new'* truth concerning Nietzsche's target audience. Far from opposing the ascetic ideal, these 'knowers' are among its last remaining champions. Nietzsche invites them to join him in hosting the final act in the self-destruction of Christian morality.

Sections 23–26: Examination of science as an alternative to, or opponent of, the ascetic ideal.

Section 26 is presented as a polemical digression from the main narrative, wherein Nietzsche fulminates against modern historiographers and other purveyors of sham ideals.

Section 27: Explanation of the historical procession thus far of the self-destruction of Christian morality, with particular emphasis on the opportunity for Nietzsche and his readers to make the will to truth conscious of itself as a problem.

Section 28: Recapitulation of the main narrative, with particular emphasis on the *will to nothingness* that ascetic ideals both shelter and express.

CHAPTER 3

READING THE TEXT

PROLOGUE

Section 1

The first word of the Preface to GM is 'We' [*Wir*]. This may strike some readers as an odd way for Nietzsche to begin his exposé of Western morality, especially if they know him primarily as a champion of heroic individualism. While Nietzsche's high regard for the heroic exploits of singular individuals is well known, GM positions us to understand that his more basic concern is with the ways in which *culture* determines one's prospects for leading an authentic individual existence. Individuals thus emerge, if at all, from the larger 'we' in which they receive their habituation and acculturation. As we shall see, in fact, it is only as a member of a 'we' that Nietzsche can conduct his assault on Christian morality – hence his appeal in this section to like-minded readers who may share his destiny.

The 'we' for whom he speaks in this section is notable for its pursuit of knowledge, to be sure, but also for its impressive lack of self-understanding. The 'knowers'[1] whom he addresses in GM are in fact 'strangers' to themselves, in large part because it has never occurred to them to suspend their knowledge-gathering routine long enough to get to know themselves. Far from objecting to their self-estrangement, moreover, they accept it as if it were a law that 'applies to all eternity'. Lacking both the 'earnestness' and the 'time' needed to attend to their own 'so-called "experiences"', they occupy themselves with the routine task of gathering knowledge and 'bringing [it] home'. For them, it would seem, ignorance (with respect to themselves) is bliss.

Rather than chastise these 'knowers' for their lack of self-understanding, Nietzsche charitably describes them as 'divinely preoccupied', as if they had better things to do than reflect upon their own experiences. They have not managed to find themselves, he concedes, but only because they 'have never sought' themselves, which in their case is a very good thing. Unlike those philosophers who happily take their place in the venerable lineage of Socrates, Nietzsche refuses to issue any general affirmation of the hoary quest for self-knowledge. As he explains elsewhere,

> where *nosce te ipsum* [know thyself] would be the recipe for ruin, forgetting oneself, *misunderstanding* oneself . . . [would] become reason itself. (EH: 'clever' 9)

As this extract suggests, Nietzsche is unusually attentive to the perils involved in any unauthorized, or premature, quest for self-knowledge. That he sees fit to rouse these unsuspecting 'knowers' thus attests to the urgency of the educational programme in which he intends to enrol them. As we shall see, in fact, he addresses these kindred 'knowers', interrupting their established routines, because he cannot afford to wait for them to awaken on their own to the destiny that he suspects they share with him.

Although he does not elaborate here on the basis for his sympathetic identification with these 'knowers', we may conclude from what he says elsewhere that he regards their lack of self-understanding as a promising sign of the unseen development under way within them. He thus interprets their *need* to misunderstand themselves as evidence that a 'great prudence' is silently at work in them, protecting them from the 'ruin' of self-knowledge until they are fully prepared to assume the burden of their 'task' (EH: 'clever' 9). As he explains throughout his Preface to GM, he knows this about them because his own development has followed a similar course and trajectory. Having already travelled the path that lies ahead of them, he offers to lead them on their maiden voyage of self-discovery. Unlike him, they will have the benefit of a seasoned guide as they navigate their passage from innocence to experience.

If they are to follow his lead, of course, they will need to become more than the 'knowers' described in this section. In their quest for knowledge, which Nietzsche likens to the back-and-forth flight of the honey-gatherer, they have been concerned thus far simply with 'bringing something home'. This means, as he explains else-where, that they gather knowledge by assimilating something new, foreign, distant or strange to something that is already familiar to them (GS 355). To 'bring something home', he thus implies, is to take what is already familiar as the measure of what one can and should know.

Nietzsche has no wish to register a general objection to this par-ticular approach to the pursuit of knowledge. For most of us, most of the time, 'bringing something home' is perfectly adequate to our needs. Our adherence to what is already familiar furthermore pro-tects us from the unexpected surprises and injuries that are likely to arise from prolonged contact with something new and strange. As an approach to gathering knowledge, in fact, 'bringing something home' becomes problematic only in the event that one wishes to know more about what is already most familiar, e.g. the 'treasure' that one hoards, or the 'home' in which one stores it. As Nietzsche explains elsewhere,

> What is familiar is what we are used to: and what we are used to is most difficult to 'know' – that is, to see as a problem; that is, to see as strange, as distant, as 'outside us'. (GS 355)

To most seekers of knowledge, of course, it would make no sense to aspire to see something familiar 'as a problem'. As we have seen, the whole point of seeking knowledge is to assimilate the 'strange' and 'distant' to what is already familiar to us.

Here it becomes clear that Nietzsche means to address GM to those rare 'knowers' who are prepared to investigate what is most familiar to them. Rather than simply 'bring something home', he hopes, they will agree to join him in seeing morality itself 'as a problem'. In order to do so, however, they must first attain a critical distance from morality, such that it might appear, for the first time, unfamiliar to them. Once they gain the critical distance they need, they may join Nietzsche in assessing the *genuine* value of morality, which, until now, they have simply taken for granted.

Section 2

In this section, Nietzsche launches his account of his own develop-ment as a genealogist of morals. As we have seen, this story is meant to convince his readers that he has already travelled the path that lies ahead of them, and that he would therefore be a reliable and trust-worthy guide.

Employing his favourite image of fecundity, the tree, he reveals the 'common root' of his ideas on morality, which, he believes, accounts for the continuity of his most recent efforts with his earliest thoughts on the subject. Anticipating his sketch in Essay III of the fruitful, 'maternal' philosopher, he cautions his readers, whom he addresses as fellow 'philosophers', not to be distracted by others' opinions of the 'fruit' they bear. His wish for his readers is that they, like fruit-bearing trees, gravid mothers and inspired artists, will find adequate justification for their creative endeavours in the 'evidence' they furnish 'of *one* will, *one* health, *one* soil, *one* sun'.

Section 3

Wishing to disclose the necessity that has guided his own development as a philosopher, Nietzsche reluctantly calls attention to the 'scruple' that 'entered [his] life so early' and predisposed him to be so relentlessly sceptical of morality. An early expression of this scepticism led him to confer upon God the 'honour' of being 'the *father* of evil'. Later on, having learned not 'to look for the origin of evil behind the world', he began to refine the aggressively naturalistic line of inquiry that characterizes his approach in GM:

> [U]nder what conditions did human beings devise these value judgments good and evil? *And what value do they themselves possess?*

On the strength of this methodological breakthrough, he soon discovered that his investigation of morality had yielded 'an entire discrete, thriving, flourishing world, like a secret garden the existence of which no one suspected'. Much to his surprise, he had acquired a 'country', a 'soil', all his own, which he now invites his readers to explore with him.

Section 4

Continuing his autobiographical sketch, he draws his readers' attention to his previous inquiries into the history of morality. He refers in particular to his book *Human, All-Too-Human* (1878), in part so that he might also introduce his readers to his presumed rivals. This book was written in response to *The Origin of the Moral Sensations* (1877), whose author, Dr Paul Rée (1849–1901), was at the time Nietzsche's close friend.[2] According to Nietzsche, Rée's book features 'an upside-down and perverse species of genealogical hypothesis', which is representative of 'the genuinely *English* type'. By way of contrast, he draws his readers' attention to the superior, unsentimental explanations that his own books provide of the moral phenomena under investigation in GM.

An alternative autobiographical sketch of this period, pertaining to Nietzsche's purported *convalescence*, is found in the new Prefaces that he appends to the 1886 editions of *The Birth of Tragedy*, *Human, All-Too-Human* (Parts I and II), *Dawn* and *The Gay Science*. He relates a similar story of recovery in the first chapter ('Why I Am so Wise') of *Ecce Homo*, which was written in 1888. A comparison of these sketches reveals that he associates the refinement of his genealogical approach with his return to health following a life-threatening illness. The general lesson to be gleaned from these sketches is that the Nietzschean practice of genealogy presupposes a degree of health that is lacking in most would-be historians of morality. This is why Nietzsche is so attentive in GM to the education and refinement of his readers' senses. The truths on offer in GM are available only to those who possess a fully functional sensory array and a strong, resilient physical constitution.

Section 5

While Rée and others contented themselves with 'hypothesis-mongering', Nietzsche proceeded to conduct a more serious – and unprecedented – inquiry into the *value* of morality'. He was especially keen to reckon the genuine value of those 'unegoistic' instincts – he mentions *pity*, *self-abnegation*, and *self-sacrifice* – to which his 'great teacher', the philosopher Arthur Schopenhauer (1788–1860) had pledged his allegiance.

This section conveys Nietzsche's understanding of morality as inextricably bound up with the unquestioned (and unwarranted) priority of the 'unegoistic' instincts, in which he was the first to detect 'the *great* danger to humankind'. Indeed, the unquestioned triumph of altruism over egoism signalled to him 'the beginning of the end'. Nietzsche thus serves notice in this section that an enduring focus of his critique of morality will be its unquestioned 'overestimation' of *pity* and all related unegoistic instincts. The 'predilection for pity' is particularly irksome to Nietzsche, for it is by means of pity that morality makes suffering 'contagious' and thereby expands the sphere of its dominion (A 7).

Section 6

His break with Schopenhauer was decisive, he now explains, for on the strength of his repudiation of pity, 'a tremendous new prospect open[ed] up' for him. As he yielded to his vertiginous 'mistrust' of morality, a 'new demand' became 'audible' to him:

> [W]e need a *critique* of moral values, *the value of these values themselves must first be called in question*—³

His reception of this new demand in turn prompted him to develop and employ a novel approach to the history of morality. This approach is meant to disclose the unacknowledged – and largely unimagined – historical background of the moral values under scrutiny. Before the value of moral values can be called into question, he realized, we first need to understand 'the conditions and circumstances under which they grew, under which they evolved and changed'. In order to seek this kind of preliminary knowledge, of course, one must be open to the possibility that values do in fact grow, evolve and change. As we shall see, he is particularly concerned in GM to demonstrate the contingency and mutability of those values that his rivals insist on regarding as permanent and unchanging.

In a rhetorical flourish that betrays his own extra-scholarly sympathies, he links the urgency of this critique to the alarming rate at which morality threatens to dispossess us. By propping up the increasingly unsupportable 'good individual', morality funds the present '*at the expense of the future*'. In undertaking this critique, he thus cautions, we must be prepared not only to discover that morality has actually *prevented* humanity from attaining 'its *highest power and splendor and power*', but also to conclude that 'precisely morality was the danger of dangers'. Here it may be helpful to bear in mind that Nietzsche regards *danger* as the single most effective catalyst of growth and development (TI 9: 38). Introducing his readers to the unprecedented danger that morality represents thus positions them to develop the resources they will need if they are to join him in his assault on Christian morality.

Section 7

Hoping to recruit 'scholarly, bold, and industrious comrades' who would assist him in surveying the recently disclosed 'land of morality',[4] Nietzsche invited the aforementioned Dr Rée to join him. But Dr Rée declined, opting instead to continue to 'gaze around haphazardly in the blue'.

As Nietzsche now reconstructs this slight, he attributes Dr Rée's response to the latter's misreading and misappropriation of Darwin's theory of natural selection. Convinced that the process of human evolution has followed a relatively tame and uneventful course, such that we moderns might 'politely link hands' with the brutes from which we are descended, Dr Rée saw no point in taking seriously the 'problems of morality' that exercise Nietzsche in GM. Signalling that he does not share Dr Rée's placid understanding of human evolution, Nietzsche declares that he regards nothing to be worthier of serious attention than these problems. 'Among the rewards' for taking them seriously, he explains, is that 'some day one will perhaps be allowed to take them *cheerfully*.' He thus recommends his novel genealogical approach not only for its seriousness, but also for that which his seriousness soon may yield: his *cheerfulness*, which he associates with the practice of 'the gay science'.

Although Nietzsche finds cheerfulness attractive in its own right, it is important to him in this context in so far as it provides a reliable index of renewed strength and renascent health. The only 'proof of strength', he explains elsewhere, is its 'excess', which may take the form of the 'cheerfulness' with which one approaches a 'gloomy affair, fraught with immeasurable responsibility' (TI P).[5] We will know that we are strong, that is, when we are able and willing to take cheerfully those questions and problems that we also take most seriously. Taking seriously these problems of morality, he thus suggests, will make us stronger, and the renewal of our strength will liberate us in turn from the leaden, earthbound gravity of our seriousness. Although he presents himself here as not yet having earned his full 'reward', he is nevertheless able to accent his genealogical inquiries with transient bursts of cheerfulness. As we shall see, his good cheer enables him to hypothesize – and subsequently to document – moments of genuine difference in the developmental history of morality. Unlike Dr Rée, that is, he traces our descent from genuine brutes, with whom we would not dare to 'link hands'.

Nietzsche's reference in this section to the 'reward' of cheerfulness also forges a thematic link between his project in GM and his larger campaign to sponsor an affirmative response to the 'death of God'. Although he makes no explicit reference in GM to the 'death of God', he suggests in other writings that the 'death of God' furnishes both the historical context and the urgency of his project in GM. As we shall see, in fact, he interprets the palpable decline of faith in the Christian God as presenting him (and his best readers) with a *'new problem'*, which they will attempt to solve, or so he proposes, by conducting an unprecedented critique of truth itself (GM III: 24).

As he explains elsewhere, the 'death of God' refers not to the demise of an actual deity, but to a growing crisis of confidence in the basic belief structure that supports our system of morality. Attendant on this erosion of credibility is the impending 'collapse' of the 'whole of our European morality' (GS 343). By announcing the 'death of God', that is, Nietzsche means to herald the end of the moral period of human history and the dawning, perhaps, of an extra-moral period of human history. That others are as yet oblivious to the 'death of God' is perfectly understandable, he explains, for the full meaning of this event is not yet generally available:

> The event itself is far too great, too distant, too remote from the multitude's capacity for comprehension even for the tidings of it to be thought of as having *arrived* as yet. (GS 343)

In contrast to the multitude, Nietzsche and his unnamed companions know that God is dead. What is more, they have embraced the death of God as a positive, liberating event, even as they acknowledge the 'long plenitude and sequence of breakdown, destruction, ruin, and cataclysm that is now impending' (GS 343). As the title of this passage suggests, in fact, 'the meaning of [their] cheerfulness' is to be found in their affirmative response thus far to the death of God (GS 343). That they are cheerful, he believes, means that they no longer require the support and reinforcement that belief in a divine order once provided. Their cheerfulness thus attests to the return of their strength and health, which explains why they are now free to explore the 'open sea' that lies before them (GS 343).

With this discussion in mind, let us turn now to consider the concluding sentences of Section 7 of his Preface to GM. In these sentences, Nietzsche implies that the 'reward' to which our serious labours entitle us will involve the recognition that 'our own morality too is part *of the comedy*'. On such a day, we (or our heirs) will come to see morality for what it is and always has been – namely, as a finite act within a larger 'drama', scripted by 'the grand old eternal comic poet of our existence'. Although whimsically expressed, this reference to a pagan deity accurately reflects Nietzsche's preference for divine spectators who display an unending, if occasionally cruel, fascination with human affairs. As this reference suggests, in fact, the future of humankind would be far more secure if we were in a position to blame the gods not only for our moral failings, but also for the failings of morality itself.

Section 8

Nietzsche closes his Preface by refusing full responsibility for any failure on the part of his readers to understand GM. In a book devoted to the origins of guilt, debt and responsibility, he questions whether the guilt necessarily lies with him if a particular reader does not understand GM.

In this final section of the Preface, Nietzsche also reveals his assumption that prospective readers of GM have 'first read [his] earlier writings and [have] not spared some trouble in doing so'. As we shall see, he relies throughout GM on these earlier writings, which are clearly integral to the case he wishes to build against morality. He then recommends several diagnostic tests that might determine how well his readers have understood his earlier writings. Anyone who claims really to 'know' his *Zarathustra*, for example, should 'at some time [have] been profoundly wounded and at some time profoundly delighted by every word in it'. His more aphoristic writings, he continues, call for both 'exegesis' and a corresponding 'art of exegesis', the mastery of which will oblige his readers to cultivate the forgotten habit of 'rumination'. As we shall see, GM itself goes a long way toward training its target audience in the prescribed art of reading. Despite the urgency of his rhetoric, in fact, Nietzsche implores the readers of GM to *slow down* as they read, reflect, speak and prepare themselves for the future.[6]

Study questions

1. What is the nature of the 'we' to which Nietzsche addresses himself in the Preface to GM?

2. What 'new demand' eventually became 'audible' to Nietzsche as he investigated the value of morality?
3. Why would Nietzsche consider *morality* to be 'the danger of dangers'?
4. Why does Nietzsche take so seriously the problems of morality?

ESSAY I: 'GOOD AND EVIL', 'GOOD AND BAD'

Section 1

Nietzsche begins Essay I on a conciliatory note. As it turns out, the English psychologists, whom he lampooned in his Preface, are in fact '*interesting*'. He is fascinated in particular by their tendency to retrieve only the shameful bits from 'our inner world', which they subsequently describe in the least flattering terms available to them. While this tendency no doubt betrays the misanthropy that motivates their research, Nietzsche hopefully speculates that it also reflects a determination

> to sacrifice all desirability to truth, *every* truth, even plain, harsh, ugly, repellent, unchristian, immoral truth.

If such were the case, he implies, he would be happy to count the English psychologists as potential allies in his campaign to disclose the undesirable truth about morality.

Whatever else they might be, the English psychologists are useful to Nietzsche. He is obliged to them not only for their groundbreaking research, but also for provoking him to respond with such creative ferocity. Despite his well-known antipathy for the operation of reactive forces, in fact, he is often at his best in GM when reacting to the flawed views of his rivals.[7] This is why, in the end, he cannot simply dismiss the English psychologists. As we shall see very clearly in the next section, their provocations are indispensable to the rhetorical-dramatic structure of GM and to the general progress of his genealogy of morals.

Section 2

Having identified the English psychologists as potentially kindred spirits, Nietzsche now alleges that they are altogether lacking in the '*historical spirit* itself'. That is, they are unable to investigate the past without first projecting onto it the values, prejudices and pieties of the present. In general, what they claim to find in the past is nothing more than the cluster of anachronisms that they typically import, unwittingly, into the sites of their investigations. As a result, their genealogical explanations invariably fail to retrieve any evidence of values and moralities significantly different from their own. In order to explain the historical persistence of their own values, of course, they are obliged to devise wildly inventive and implausible theories.

This lack of historical spirit is particularly conspicuous in their attempts to explain the origin of the concept (and corresponding judgement) of *good*. Having traced the origin of this concept to what was originally considered *useful*, they insist that, over time, this original relationship (between *good* and *useful*) was forgotten. So it was, they claim, that 'unegoistic actions', which were originally deemed *good* on the basis of their utility for those who benefited from them, eventually came to be deemed *good* on the basis, as it were, of their intrinsic value. This is how the English psychologists account for the priority that is generally assigned to those actions that are regarded as *selfless* (or *unegoistic*), especially in comparison to those actions that are regarded as *selfish* (or *egoistic*).

Nietzsche raises two objections to this derivation. First, the English psychologists are simply mistaken to assume that 'the judgment "good" . . . originate[d] with those to whom "goodness" was shown'. (As we shall see, this particular mistake is typical of Nietzsche's rivals.) He consequently proposes an alternative derivation, which traces the 'origin of the antithesis "good" and "bad" ' to the experience of ' "the good" themselves', and, more precisely, to the expression of the *pathos* of distance that informs the hierarchical structure of an aristocratic society. According to Nietzsche, that is, the concepts (and corresponding judgements) of *good* and *bad* originated with those 'noble, powerful, high-stationed and high-minded' individuals who called themselves and everything related to them *good*, while reserving the term *bad* for everyone and everything else. As we shall see, in fact, nothing is more characteristically noble than the untroubled experience of oneself as belonging to a 'higher ruling order in relation to a lower order'.

He concludes from this alternative derivation that the concept of *good* was not originally associated with values or actions that we might call *altruistic* (or *unegoistic*). The designation *good* instead originated with the nobles' selfish (or egoistic) assertion of their own incomparable self-worth and unrivalled social station. Inasmuch as they deemed themselves *good* and everyone else *bad*, moreover, they were profoundly disinclined to show goodness to anyone who might find it useful, as the English psychologists allege. Nietzsche thus associates the currency of the popular opposition between egoistic and unegoistic actions with the *decline* of 'aristocratic value judgments' and the concomitant ascendancy of the '*herd instinct*'. In doing so, he offers a preliminary solution to the riddle of the English psychologists. Unable to see beyond the horizon of their own herd-centred values, they are only able to detect and process evidence that is suggestive of unegoistic value judgements. Their own aversion to the egoistic values of a noble aristocracy thus prevents them from entertaining any hypothesis that would place these values at the centre of a thriving culture, people or morality. Thus we see that Nietzsche's chief advantage over his rival genealogists is his openness to the possibility that values other than our own have been integral to the development of morality.

Section 3

Turning now to his second objection, he insists that the derivation proffered by the English psychologists 'suffers from an inherent psychological absurdity'. If the goodness of unegoistic actions were known to be a function of their utility, he wonders, would this simple, species-preserving fact not have been designated for permanent memorialization? The utility of these actions could have been forgotten, he counters, only in the event that it actually expired 'at some time or other'. Clearly, however, 'the opposite is the case', for the utility of unegoistic actions has become nearly impossible to forget. The irony here is that Nietzsche regards the utility of unegoistic actions as both grossly exaggerated *and* indelibly imprinted – or nearly so – onto human consciousness.

A 'much more reasonable' explanation, he believes, is offered by Herbert Spencer (1820–1903), who similarly proposed to derive *goodness* from *utility*. According to Spencer, the 'judgments "good" and "bad"' are meant to attest to the '*unforgotten* and *unforgettable* experiences of humankind', which provide us with an indispensable almanac of 'what is useful-practical and what is harmful-impractical'. On Spencer's account, moral designations like *good* and *bad* thus function as a kind of shorthand notation for those virtues, values and actions that are most (or least) conducive to human progress and flourishing. While this explanation avoids the psychological absurdity described above, Spencer too travels the 'wrong' road, for he too traces the origin of the concept *good* to the experience of those for whom goodness proved to be useful.

Section 4

Having registered his objections, Nietzsche turns now to defend his alternative derivation of the concept of *good*. 'The signpost to the *right* road,' he explains, became apparent to him by virtue of his study of various linguistic designations for the concept *good*, all of which attest, he claims, to 'the *same conceptual transformation*'. He thus maintains that

> '[N]oble,' 'aristocratic' in the social sense, is the basic concept from which 'good' in the sense of 'with aristocratic soul,' 'noble,' . . . necessarily developed.

He detects a parallel development with respect to the transformation of concepts denoting low social standing (e.g. 'common', 'plebeian') into concepts denoting a vulgar or base moral condition (e.g. 'bad'). He thus concludes that the origins of the *moral* designations under investigation can and should be traced to the *pre-moral* (i.e. social and political) designations from which they are derived.[8]

He pronounces this insight *fundamental* to the correct practice of 'moral genealogy', and he attributes its belated arrival on the scene to the 'retarding influence exercised by the democratic prejudice in the modern world toward all questions of origin'. Elaborating on his earlier indictment of the poor in (historical) spirit (GM I: 1), he now identifies the cause or source of their poverty. Whereas he is able to escape the gravitational pull of the democratic prejudice, his predecessors and rivals have no choice but to discover common and plebeian forces presiding over the birth and ascendancy of all values. At all costs, this prejudice asserts, we should avoid finding the origins of our highest values in a past that honoured non- and anti-democratic values, for any such derivation would call into question the *value* of our values – even to the point of interpreting the currency of the democratic prejudice as a symptom of cultural decline. Any solution to the riddle of the English psychologists must therefore take into consideration their inability to resist the thrall of the democratic prejudice.

Section 5

Including his readers for the first time in the narrative of Essay I, Nietzsche refers to 'our problem', which he identifies (in contrast to the volcanic *plebeianism* of Buckle) as a 'quiet problem', audible 'to few ears'. Having flattered his readers, he now proceeds to elaborate on the fundamental insight recorded in the previous section.

Although noble individuals most often 'designate themselves simply by their superiority in power', they also do so by citing those '*typical character traits*' that distinguish them from the lower orders of society. Here Nietzsche narrows the focus of his etymological investigation to a consideration of those traits that noble types have regarded as emblematic of their elevated rank and status. As an example, he charts the transformation of the concept that was used by the Greek nobility to designate its superior social station. Originally, he explains, the designation of oneself as *good* was meant to call attention to oneself as 'one who *is*, who possesses reality, who is actual, who is true'. Later, as the designation acquired a more subjective connotation, it was meant to call attention to oneself as 'truthful', as distinguished from 'the *lying*, common man'. Finally, following the decline of the nobility, *good* came to 'designate nobility of soul', independent of the material and social conditions that are typically associated with aristocracy. Only then did ignoble individuals dare to refer to themselves as *good*. They did so, as Nietzsche has hinted, not on the basis of a selfish, egoistic affirmation of their incomparable self-worth, but on the basis of their selfless, unegoistic deference to others, as evidenced by their experience of suffering and deprivation.

As this example is meant to demonstrate, our close attention to the etymology of moral terms and concepts may enable us to discern traces of a bygone noble morality, wherein the value assigned to unegoistic values was by no means positive.

Section 6

Summarizing his argument thus far, Nietzsche presents the following 'rule' of conceptual transformation:

> a concept denoting political superiority always resolves itself into a concept denoting superiority of soul.

As we have seen, this process of resolution also reflects the fall of the nobility whose superiority the concept formerly signified. As the political and material fortunes of the nobles decline, their preferred designations of themselves become ever more closely associated with internal states and virtues, for which little external, physical evidence is required. These designations thus become ripe for appropriation by ignoble others. If noble deeds and exploits are no longer expected in support of these designations, then anyone – including, as we shall see, a slave – may refer to himself by means of designations that formerly denoted a superior social standing. This process of resolution thus yields concepts that are ever more abstract and general, which means that they are progressively better suited to denote superiority of soul.

Having articulated this rule and broached the topic of the decline of the nobility, Nietzsche is now prepared to develop the guiding thesis of Essay I: The designation *good* originated with the *noble morality* and only later, after the decline of the nobility, became associated with the *slave morality*, from which contemporary morality is descended. In developing this thesis, Nietzsche places his alternative derivation of the concept of *good* in the background of the more familiar derivation. Long before unselfish actions were deemed *good* by those who benefited from them, he maintains, selfish actions were deemed *good* by the noble individuals who performed them. In itself, of course, this claim does not demonstrate that the noble morality was or is preferable to the slave morality. For that claim, Nietzsche will need to make a separate argument.

He then turns to consider the potentially exceptional case of an aristocratic society in which 'the highest caste is at the same time the *priestly* caste'. In such societies, he explains, the concepts of *pure* and *impure* not only designate social stations, but also reflect the distance that separates the stations they designate. According to the aforementioned rule of conceptual transformation, the pre-moral designations *pure* and *impure* naturally resolve themselves into familiar moral designations – a *good* and a *bad* – that are assigned independent of social station. Here Nietzsche reminds his readers that his narrative has not yet exited the aristocratic domain of 'good and bad'. Both forms of aristocracy – the knightly and the priestly – display the unmistakably noble evaluations that are indicative of the *pathos* of distance. As we shall see, in fact, neither caste is friendly either to the lower orders of society or to one another. Their enmity for each other is apparently a simple matter of their competing (and mutually exclusive) claims to nobility. Neither caste is willing to accept a subordinate position in the social hierarchy.

Nietzsche wastes little time placing his cards on the table. He does not care for the priestly type, and he identifies the priestly caste as an insidious threat to its knightly counterpart, which he clearly favours. He thus introduces the priests not with reference to their social role or religious function, but, anticipating his analysis in Essay III, as a *physiological* type, which he associates with sickliness and degeneration.[9] While he is careful to note the 'intestinal morbidity and neurasthenia which has afflicted priests at all times', he is far more concerned to expose the 'remedy' the priests have prescribed to themselves – namely, their cultivation of habits 'which turn them away from action and alternate between brooding and emotional explosions'. He thus regards the priests as both pathologically averse to action and alarmingly inexpert at diagnosing the illness that afflicts them. Owing to these twin defects, in fact, the remedy they have prescribed to themselves has turned out to be 'a hundred times more dangerous in its effects than the sickness it was supposed to cure'. This is the case, as we shall see, because the priests have prescribed their remedy to others, for whom it has been similarly disastrous. He thus identifies the priestly aristocracy as a site of self-inflicted instability, to which he traces the structural deformation that was exploited by the instigators of the slave revolt in morality.

Despite his low regard for the priestly type, Nietzsche nevertheless concludes this section with an important concession:

> [I]t was on the soil of this *essentially dangerous* form of human existence, the priestly form, that man became an *interesting animal*, that only here did the human soul in a higher sense acquire *depth* and become *evil* – and these are the two basic respects in which humankind has hitherto been superior to other beasts.

As we shall see, he hopes to show that the toxic influence of the priests has in fact delivered humankind to the threshold of an extramoral period in its history. While his polemic encourages us to regard the priests as villains, that is, his genealogical narrative suggests that they may yet turn out to be the secret heroes of this as-yet-unfinished story. In any event, he means for us to understand that the influence of the priests plays a key role in the developmental account he wishes to defend.

Section 7

In light of this diagnosis of the priestly type, we should not be surprised to learn that conflict between the priestly and knightly-aristocratic modes of evaluation is inevitable. Here Nietzsche hypothesizes an unstable political system in which the priestly and warrior castes vie for power and pride of place. As these two castes gravitate toward poles of mutual opposition, the differences between their respective modes of evaluation appear in progressively sharper relief.

The prospect of conflict between these two castes affords Nietzsche the opportunity to identify the physiological preconditions of the knightly-aristocratic mode of valuation:

> a powerful physicality, a flourishing, abundant, even overflowing health, together with that which serves to preserve it: war, adventure, hunting, dancing, war games, and in general all that involves vigorous, free, joyful activity.

By way of contrast, the value judgements of the priestly caste presuppose inwardness, abstinence, self-deprivation and an aversion to action. If the conflict between these two castes were to escalate into overt, violent warfare, the overwhelming advantage would fall to the knightly-aristocratic caste.

Rather than document the certain victory of the noble warriors, however, Nietzsche abruptly shifts the focus of his narrative to the *priests*, whom he identifies, somewhat cryptically, as 'the *most evil enemies*'. His recourse to this particular designation is noteworthy, for he regards it as the 'basic concept' and signature 'creation' of the slave morality (GM I: 10). Whereas the slave morality reserves this designation for those who are most potent (namely, the knightly nobles), Nietzsche assigns it here to those who are least potent (namely, the priests). The secret of priestly power, he thus intimates, is that it arises unexpectedly from a more basic condition of powerlessness. 'The priests are the *most evil enemies*', he thus explains, because their impotence produces in them a hatred of unrivalled toxicity, which they are able to replicate in others. What is particularly frightening about priestly hatred is that it targets for destruction everything upon which the priest's power – which is exclusively reactive – is dependent. This means, as we shall see, that the priest is no ordinary enemy, for he holds nothing in reserve.[10] He attacks his enemies not to aggrandize himself, but simply to eradicate all manifestations of the health, power and strength that occasion his resentment.[11] That the priest thereby destroys the conditions of his own existence is evidence of the *will to nothingness* that animates his ministry.

Armed with this insight, we are now prepared to fill the gap in Nietzsche's narrative. When faced with the prospect of war with the knightly nobles, the impotent priests responded, as was their habit, by turning inward. Their hatred of the knightly nobles grew 'to monstrous and uncanny proportions', until it finally yielded the weapons and strategies that would allow the priests to prevail in a war of cunning. In particular, as we shall see, their hatred grew to the point of becoming productive of new values, including, most notably, the invention of the *evil enemy* (GM I: 10). Here we might speculate that Nietzsche neither documents nor celebrates the victory of the knightly warriors because this victory set in motion the doomsday machinery of priestly revenge. In subduing the priests, that is, the knightly caste unwittingly sowed the seeds of its own destruction, even as it launched human history along a far more interesting – and dangerous – trajectory of development.

Changing course a second time, Nietzsche abruptly turns to consider the Jews, 'that priestly people', to whom he attributes 'an act of the *most spiritual revenge*' – namely, an *inversion* of the aristocratic values that had sustained the noble peoples and nations of antiquity.[12] Against all odds, the Jews pursued this inversion until it actually yielded an alternative 'value-equation'. Content for now not to name the heirs of the Jewish inversion of aristocratic values – even though his paraphrase of the Beatitudes leaves no doubt who he has in mind – Nietzsche declares that 'with the Jews there begins *the slave revolt in morality*'.

Section 8

Wondering if his readers can discern the victory of the slaves, Nietzsche concedes that 'all *protracted* things are hard to see, to see whole'. As if to assist those readers whose hyperopic vision fails them, he helps himself once again to the arboreal imagery that he occasionally employs in GM. Here he identifies 'Jewish hatred' as the 'trunk' of the tree of Western morality, from which sprouted 'a *new love*', as promised and practised by Christianity, which remains as yet unnamed in the narrative.[13] As this imagery implies, he understands Christian morality as an organic outgrowth of the priestly hatred that he associates with the Jews. Inasmuch as this hatred is directed against those fortunate, well-born, self-assured warriors of the knightly-aristocratic caste, he means to suggest here that Christianity too is opposed to all things noble. What Jews and Christians share in common, he thus wishes to assert, is precisely the slave revolt in morality, which began with the priestly Jews of the Second Temple Period and attained its full fruition under the 'sign' of Christian morality.

Nietzsche thus portrays Christian love as the refinement and perfection of priestly Jewish hatred. He goes so far as to allege that 'Jesus of Nazareth', the 'ostensible opponent and disintegrator of Israel', was in fact secretly *employed* by Israel as 'the instrument of its revenge'. This reference to Jesus as the 'Redeemer', whose 'incarnate gospel of love' was twisted into a hateful teaching of revenge, is meant to implicate Paul (*c*.3–*c*.65), the apostle to the Gentiles, whom Nietzsche regarded as the true founder of Christianity. According to Nietzsche, in fact, it was Paul who dangled Jesus before 'the opponents of Israel', precisely so that they 'could unhesitatingly swallow just this bait' and thereby ingest the poison of Christian morality. Under the (still unnamed) 'sign' of Christianity, he thus declares, 'Israel . . . has hitherto triumphed again and again . . . over all *nobler* ideals.' This allusion to the conversion of Emperor Constantine (*c*.285–337) confirms that the slave revolt extended into the fourth century CE,[14] at which point Christianity had become an established religion within the Roman Empire.

This section also reveals the likely point of Nietzsche's recourse to the potentially inflammatory anti-Semitic rhetoric that inflects Essay I.[15] Those Christians who wish to see themselves as opponents of Judaism are now obliged to regard themselves as more perfectly evolved practitioners of the priestly hatred that Nietzsche earlier attributed to the Jews (GM I: 7). Here we see, in fact, that much of the blame that Nietzsche heaps upon the Jews in Essay I is more fairly apportioned to the early Christians, in whom the hatred of nobility rose to an unrivalled pitch of severity.[16] Indeed, Nietzsche's use of anti-Semitic rhetoric may be meant to disclose the disconcerting truth that Christian anti-Semitism is in fact a complicated expression of *self*-hatred.

Section 9

Nietzsche devotes this section to an interlude, in which he relates the response of a hypothetical 'free spirit' to his account of the slave revolt in morality. At least at first glance, this free spirit appears quite credible (or 'honest', as Nietzsche remarks), for he does not attach any sentimental value to a bygone culture or toppled empire that he happens to favour. In general, moreover, the designation of *free spirit* is among the highest that Nietzsche bestows upon his fellow human beings, although, as we shall see, it also connotes a certain lack of self-understanding (GM III: 24).

This free spirit wishes, honourably, to 'stick to the facts'. He thus claims to accept Nietzsche's account of the slave revolt in morality as an explanation of the progress of European civilization. He has no further use for the church, which he regards as little more than a system for delivering the 'poison' that 'we' have learned to 'love', and he apparently intends his rejection of theism as a declaration of independence from faith in all its forms. Equating 'progress' with the simple movement of history, he is understandably unwilling to consider Nietzsche's suggestion that the movement of history often describes a descending arc. The values and ideals that have prevailed, he apparently means to claim, are simply those that *ought* to have prevailed.

Clearly, however, the matter is not as simple as this free spirit wishes to believe. First of all, his fidelity to the 'facts' is at best selective. That humankind has thus far *survived* the slave revolt in morality is by no means proof that this process of 'intoxication' has been *successful*. Second, he conveniently misplaces his positivism when *he* wishes to discriminate between what is (e.g. the 'crude and boorish' manners of the church) and what ought to be (e.g. 'a truly modern taste'). Third, his inconsistent espousal of democratic sympathies in fact betrays his undemocratic wish to feel superior to others. He thus rejects out of hand Nietzsche's appeal to the 'nobler ideals' of antiquity, in comparison to which his own ideals pale, while confidently affirming his superiority to those who still need the church. As this last point confirms, in fact, our free spirit prefers his interpretation of the slave revolt because it presents *him* 'as the goal and zenith, as the meaning of history' (GM I: 11). As he has correctly surmised from Nietzsche's account thus far, the success or failure of the slave revolt must be reflected in him. In this light, we should not be too surprised that he insists on its complete success, even if doing so obliges him to profess his 'love' for the 'poison' he has ingested.

If this free spirit is to continue under Nietzsche's tutelage, he will need to re-examine his democratic sympathies. In particular, he will need to acknowledge that his feeling of superiority has less to do with his own achievements than with the pandemic levelling of humankind in general. As Nietzsche makes clear later on, now is not the time for 'hopelessly mediocre and insipid' human beings to celebrate their elevation above the 'ill-constituted, sickly, weary and exhausted people of which Europe is beginning to stink' (GM I: 11).

Section 10

Despite having 'much to be silent about' (GM I: 9), Nietzsche begins this section with one of the most original and explosive claims delivered in GM. Returning to his earlier discussion, he explains that

> The slave revolt in morality begins when *ressentiment* itself becomes creative and gives birth to values: the *ressentiment* of natures that are denied the true reaction, that of deeds, and compensate themselves with an imaginary revenge.

As we shall see, the slave revolt in morality was successful only because these newborn values eventually came to be embodied in the slaves who espoused them. *How* these alien values became second nature – first, to the slaves and subsequently to their oppressors – is what Nietzsche must now explain. He does not speculate here on the paternity of these new values, but we have good reason to suspect that the *ascetic priest* is the party responsible for impregnating the *ressentiment* of the slaves. Although the ascetic priest does not formally enter the narrative until Essay III, the products of his handiwork are occasionally marked in the text of GM, as in this case, by images of pregnancy, reproduction, fruition and generation. Although the priestly type is described as impotent (GM I: 7), the main narrative of GM would make little sense if the ascetic priest were not able to reproduce his values in others and to authorize them to do likewise. As we shall see, in fact, his asexual mode of reproduction is chiefly responsible for the cultural transmission of the values of the slave morality.

This section also offers Nietzsche's clearest formulation of his influential distinction between the *noble morality* and the *slave morality*.[17] For the purposes of articulating this distinction, he restricts himself in this section (and the next) to a consideration of the 'modes of valuation' from which, respectively, each of these moralities develops:

> While every noble morality grows out[18] of a triumphant affirmation of itself, slave morality from the outset says No to what is 'outside,' what is 'different,' what is 'not itself' . . .

Nietzsche's distinction between these contrasting modes of valuation is largely a matter of convenience. As such, the light it casts on the generative core of each morality is both clarifying and artificial. As he emphasizes later on (GM I: 16), we certainly should not expect to encounter contemporary examples of either morality in the purity of form described here.

Let us briefly review the most important differences between these two modes of evaluation and the moralities they produce:

- Whereas the noble morality originates in an individual's spontaneous, pre-reflective assessment of himself as *good*, the slave morality originates in an other-directed, other-negating assessment of the inherent *evil* of the slave's alleged oppressors. The noble morality subsequently deems *bad* everything that is foreign to it, while the slave morality subsequently deems itself *good*, though only derivatively, and only as an afterthought.
- The slave acquires his sense of identity only by default, and only by negating the attributes of those external aggressors whom he has deemed *evil*. The *goodness* attributed by the slave to himself is confirmed by nothing other than the (supposedly voluntary) suffering and passivity that distinguish him from his oppressors.
- Whereas the noble morality exists and expresses itself independently of the condition of the world it encounters, the slave morality 'always first needs a hostile external world'. As a result, the slave morality can never credibly wish for, much less work toward, a cessation of the hostility directed against it. The identity and avowed 'goodness' of the slave are therefore dependent on his (narcissistic) perception of himself as living under constant siege.
- Whereas the noble mode of valuation 'acts and grows spontaneously', the slavish mode of valuation is restricted in its range of actions to the domain of *reactivity*. The noble thus enjoys the satisfaction of his 'deeds', while the slave must content himself with the compensatory enjoyment of 'imaginary revenge'.

- The key to Nietzsche's insight into the psychology of the slave revolt is his emphasis on the creative role of *ressentiment*, whose 'essence' is 'the *need* to direct one's view outward instead of back to oneself'. This 'need' apparently arises from the failure of the slave to discern anything within himself that merits immediate, spontaneous affirmation. In expressing his *ressentiment* of the nobles, the slave wishes most fervently to ensure that *no one* will enjoy the privileges pertaining to nobility. The slave turns his view 'outward', that is, so that he may *negate*, and ultimately *destroy*, what he finds there. Wherever he encounters the flourishing of life, strength, health, power, beauty, permanence or nobility, he must dedicate himself to its eradication.
- That the slave is *also* reliant on the 'hostile external world' for his sense of identity illuminates the *will to nothingness* that lies at the heart of the slave morality. Inasmuch as the slave depends on the provocations of his enemies, in fact, his campaign to destroy all things noble is an indirect means of assuring his own destruction. Without any 'external stimuli' to which he might react, the slave would be powerless to act at all.
- Whereas the noble holds the slave in *contempt*, the slave expresses *hatred* for the noble.
- Whereas practitioners of the noble morality rely more consistently and immediately on 'the perfect functioning of the regulating unconscious instincts', with which Nietzsche approvingly associates 'bold recklessness' and 'enthusiastic impulsiveness', practitioners of the slave morality (whom he now identifies as 'men of *ressentiment*')[19] are distinctive in that they 'honor cleverness to a far greater degree'.[20]
- Whereas the noble individual treats his enemies with 'reverence' and 'honor', and as external measures of his own strength and nobility, the slave demonizes his 'evil' enemies and only thereby secures his derivative 'goodness'.
- The difference between the 'bad' [*schlecht*] of the noble morality and the 'evil' [*böse*] of the slave morality leads Nietzsche to conclude that the designation 'good' [*gut*], though common to both moralities, means something very different in each.

As it turns out, in fact, the individual who is deemed *evil* by the slave morality is none other than the individual who is deemed *good* by the noble morality. Nietzsche thus identifies the conception of ' "the evil enemy," "*the Evil One*"',[21] as the founding 'deed' and signal 'creation' of the slave revolt in morality. All other concepts – including the 'good one' – are derivative.

Section 11

This insight marks an important advance in the narrative of Essay I, for here Nietzsche acknowledges two competing perspectives on, and corresponding evaluations of, the practitioners of the noble morality. Whereas the nobles deem themselves *good*, the victims of their aggression pronounce them *evil*. Having earlier replaced the designation 'slave' with that of 'man of *ressentiment*', he now replaces the designation 'slave morality' with that of the 'morality of *ressentiment*'.[22] In both cases, as we shall see, the shift in terminology is meant to signal the formative influence of the priest, whose task it is to manage the *ressentiment* of the slaves. The priest performs this task, as we shall see, by forming a community of mutual aid and comfort, or *herd*, which he subsequently mobilizes in the service of his campaign to avenge himself against the knightly nobles and their signature mode of valuation.

Without endorsing the victim's perspective or mode of valuation, Nietzsche concedes that the men of *ressentiment* have good reason to deem their enemies *evil*. When returned to pre-moral conditions of 'wilderness', these noble individuals 'are not much better than uncaged beasts of prey'. (The designation *beast of prey*, which will play a significant role in Essay II, is thus introduced by Nietzsche in an attempt to make sense of the jaundiced perspective of the men of *ressentiment*.) Were one to encounter these nobles in their native wilderness, on furlough from the peace of civil society, one might naturally experience their self-avowed goodness as an expression of unalloyed beastliness. In wilderness, that is, these nobles would be virtually indistinguishable from any other species of bloodthirsty predator.

Still, a rampaging beast of prey is a far cry from the 'Evil One', and Nietzsche makes no attempt here (or elsewhere) to defend the heavily moralized perspective of the men of *ressentiment*. Immediately after reciting the atrocities performed by these wild beasts of prey, in fact, he claims to discern in 'these noble races the beast of prey, the splendid *blond beast* prowling about in search of spoils and victory'. (As if to cast doubt on the *literal* blondness of this beast, he promptly identifies the 'Roman, Arabian . . . [and] Japanese nobility' as examples of the 'beast of prey' that lurks at the heart of every noble people and culture.) His point here is that the type of human being who may be likened to a beast of prey is absolutely essential to the development of a thriving, healthy people or culture. He thus describes the aggression of the beast of prey as the 'hidden core' of any noble people, which, he insists, 'needs to erupt from time to time'. To pronounce this beast of prey *evil*, he thus implies, is to declare war on the very possibility of a noble people or culture. And, as we shall see, this is precisely what the men of *ressentiment* have done.

Here we should note that Nietzsche has quietly introduced the idea that the nobles described in this section lead a dangerously divided existence. It is only when 'they go outside, where the strange, the *stranger* is found', that they behave in such a way that invites comparison with 'uncaged beasts of prey'. This means, presumably, that an encounter with the nobles in their *other* habitat, that of civil society, would hardly lead one to take them for beasts of prey. That they must 'compensate themselves' in wilderness is itself indicative of the narrowing of the distance that separates them from their slaves, who, as we have seen, are obliged to 'compensate themselves with an imaginary revenge' (GM I: 10).

The designation *beast of prey* thus enables Nietzsche to distinguish, albeit implicitly, between two very different moments in the heyday of the noble morality. Like Hesiod, that is, he treats a single historical epoch as if it were two: 1) that of the form-giving beasts of prey, who appear before their victims as rogue forces of nature (GM II: 17); and 2) that of the part-time beasts of prey, who are reviled as the *evil enemies* of their victims.[23] The distance that separates these two moments in the heyday of the noble morality thus reflects the gradual transformation of the victims of noble aggression from *sufferers* into *sinners*. As this transformation progresses, the victims of noble aggression press ever more insistently for a thoroughly moralized interpretation of individuals and events that they had previously regarded as natural and amoral.

Although this particular line of interpretation was suggested by the ascetic priest (GM III: 20),[24] the beasts of prey unwittingly did their part to ensure its plausibility. By dividing their time between wilderness and civil society, they invited the charge, of which they eventually would convict themselves, that they were in fact free to suspend their customary predatory routines. The irony, of course, is that the weary nobles who finally inspired their enemies to pronounce them *evil* were really only weekend warriors. The competing demands of *freedom* (in wilderness) and *utility* (in civil society) had furrowed their souls and depleted their physical resources. Only occasionally did they revert to 'the innocent conscience of the beast of prey', and only within the limited context of their increasingly infrequent wilderness sabbaticals. Even as they were condemned for their 'prankish' displays of beastliness, that is, they were already at odds with themselves.

Having conceded that the 'good' individuals of the noble morality might resemble beasts of prey, Nietzsche now inquires after their fate. If 'the *meaning of all culture* is the reduction of the "human" beast of prey to a tame and civilized animal', he supposes, then it stands to reason that 'all those instincts of reaction and *ressentiment*' are in fact 'the actual *instruments of culture*'. This does not mean, however, that we are obliged to acknowledge the '*bearers* of these instincts', namely the men of *ressentiment*, as the true representatives of culture, especially inasmuch as they in fact 'represent the *regression* of humankind'. Nietzsche's point here is a bit obscure, for he does not accept the truth of the initial supposition. As we have seen, in fact, he wishes to defend an approach to culture that does not seek to tame the blond beast lurking at its core. Even if he did accept the truth of this supposition, however, he would still refuse to acknowledge the men of *ressentiment* as instruments of genuine culture, for their pro-liferation is counter-productive of culture. It would be far preferable, he insists, to live in *fear* of the 'blond beast' than to '*suffer* from humankind', which is the fate he shares in common with his readers.

Section 12

Here Nietzsche interrupts his own narrative to release an irrepress-ible 'sigh and a last hope'.[25] If he is to continue with his investiga-tion, he confides, he will need to be granted 'but *one* glance of . . . a human being who justifies *humankind* . . .' Such a human being, we have just learned, is equally likely to inspire fear and admiration.

The timing of this confession suggests that his need for refresh-ment is related to his reversal of perspectives in the previous section. There, as we recall, he adopted the standpoint of those who, through the 'venomous eye of *ressentiment*' (GM I: 11), pronounced the noble individual *evil*. This reversal of perspectives, we now learn, exacted a heavy toll, for it required Nietzsche to breathe the 'bad air' produced by degeneration and decay. Generalizing from his own experience, he now warns his readers that they too are at risk of growing 'weary' of humankind. They too will pay dearly to conduct, as eventually they must, a similar reversal of perspectives. As his confession-cum-warning indicates, in fact, the reversal of perspectives that he recommends to his readers is by no means limited to a hypothetical exercise. To adopt a foreign perspective is to take on an alien mode of embodiment, such that one may live, feel, think and suffer as the other does. In the extreme case described in the previous section, Nietzsche was obliged by his reversal of perspectives to ingest the noxious air to which the 'men of *ressentiment*' have grown accustomed.

As this section helpfully clarifies, *nihilism* names the condition that afflicts Nietzsche and the 'we' for whom he speaks. For the past 2,000 years, the dominant morality of European civilization has targeted for domestication those human beings who inspire fear in others. By eliminating the basis on which some human beings might inspire fear, however, morality has also eradicated the only basis on which humankind itself, through the exploits of its greatest exemplars, might inspire our continued 'love', 'reverence', 'hope' and a 'will' for its future. The only justification for humankind, the sole warrant for its future, thus lies in and with those beastly individuals who cannot help but strike fear in the hearts of others. As Nietzsche and his 'we' now realize, however, these individuals are nearing extinction at an alarming rate.

Section 13

Returning to his main narrative, Nietzsche resumes his explanation of how these 'good' individuals, these beasts of prey, came to be known as *evil*. Here he relates his famous parable of the birds of prey and the tender, tasty lambs. That the lambs would 'dislike' the birds of prey is certainly understandable. That their 'dislike' is sufficient to authorize a moralized 'reproach' of the birds of prey is another matter altogether. Still, Nietzsche professes to have 'no reason to find fault with the institution of [an] ideal' based on the designations of birds of prey as *evil* and lambs as *good*, provided the lambs keep these designations 'among themselves'.

What happens, however, when the private resentment of the lambs becomes the basis for the public dissemination of a new morality? While it would be laughable to apply moral designations to the grisly scene of natural predation, as if swooping raptors were free not to snatch tasty little lambs, Nietzsche is concerned to explain how precisely these kinds of designation became both possible and credible in the case of human beings. That the little lambs are depicted here as speaking only 'among themselves' suggests that a third party showed them how to translate their fantasies of revenge into a publicly traded morality. Inasmuch as these lambs later morph into the 'oppressed, downtrodden, [and] outraged', who tout their weakness as a 'voluntary achievement', we may infer the transformative influence of the priest. Although unnamed in this section, the priest is present by virtue of 'the counterfeit and self-deception of impotence', which enables the weak and downtrodden to present their essential weakness as if it were 'willed, chosen, a *deed*'.

Digressing a bit, Nietzsche exposes the signature belief-cum-mistake of the slave morality. According to the creative 'man of *ressentiment*' – here, too, we should infer the influence of the priest – the strong are *free* to be weak and are therefore *accountable* for the suffering they cause. That the weak ascribe such freedom to themselves and others is certainly understandable, for they *need* to interpret their defining weakness as if it 'were a voluntary achievement, willed, chosen, a *deed*, a *meritorious* act'. In fact, the psychological key to the slave revolt in morality is the audacious claim on the part of the slaves – coached by the priest, of course – to *prefer* their suffering which they propose as an unassailable index of their goodness. The slaves *could* retaliate if they so desired, or so their story goes, but they choose instead the righteous path of suffering and self-deprivation. As absurd as it may sound, the slaves claim to seek no compensation for the virtues they cultivate.

To rebut this claim, Nietzsche appeals to the kindred inventiveness of the 'popular mind', which typically 'separates the lightning from its flash and takes the latter for an *action*'. A similar (and similarly mistaken) duplication is performed by 'popular morality', which typically

separates strength from the expression of strength, as if there were a neutral substratum behind the strong man, which was *free* to express strength or not to do so.

Famously decreeing that 'there is no such substratum', he asserts that 'the deed is everything'. He thus alerts his readers to the dangerous possibilities lurking in the lambs' seemingly harmless claim that the bird of prey is *free* not to be predatory. This attribution of freedom positions the lambs 'to make the bird of prey *accountable* for being a bird of prey'. *How* they are able to do so is what Nietzsche now must explain.

Section 14

As if to provide evidence in support of the parable related in the previous section, Nietzsche wonders if anyone would like to 'take a look into the secret of how *ideals are made* on earth'. He chides his impatient readers and cautions them to accustom their eyes to the 'false, iridescent light' emanating from this 'dark workshop'. This venture calls for 'courage', inasmuch as it requires them to attempt a reversal of perspectives that is similar to the reversal he executed in Section 11. Their descent into the dark workshop is thus meant both to reproduce and to parody his earlier attempt to occupy the standpoint of the men of *ressentiment*.

Trading places with his readers, Nietzsche listens as his imagined respondent reports his findings. Not surprisingly, the respondent echoes Nietzsche's earlier refrain: 'Bad air! Bad air!' (GM I: 12). At Nietzsche's urging, moreover, his respondent 'opens [his] ears again' and hears how these men of *ressentiment* fashion *justice* from their 'hatred and revenge'.[26] Finally, his respondent hears something that will oblige Nietzsche to postpone the completion of his explanation, begun in GM I: 10, of how the 'good' man of the noble morality became known, even to himself, as the 'evil one' of the slave morality. According to his respondent, the smiths working below refer to their 'anticipated future bliss' – which they unambiguously understand as a form of compensation – as ' "the Last Judgment," the coming of *their* kingdom, of the "Kingdom of God" '. When one adopts the perspective of the men of *ressentiment*, that is, one discovers that they expect to be paid – and handsomely so – for their suffering and self-deprivation. This means, of course, that they do not value suffering simply for its own sake. As we shall see in Essay II, this particular twist to the story will lead Nietzsche to situate the origin and development of the notion of *responsibility* in the bloody context of the creditor–debtor relationship.

Section 15

Here Nietzsche finally turns to a consideration of distinctly Christian values. As it turns out, the virtues of *faith*, *love* and *hope* are esteemed not for their intrinsic value, but for their promise of the compensatory 'bliss' that awaits those who hunger for revenge.

The 'weak people' who were overheard in the previous section fully intend 'some day or other' to turn the tables on those who are strong, which contradicts their claim to *prefer* a life of suffering and deprivation. In fact, they endure such a life only as a precondition of the arrival, 'beyond death', of '*their* "kingdom" ', in which they will be 'eternally indemnified' for enduring their 'earthly life "in faith, in love, in hope" '. As we shall see, however, their wish to be paid in afterworldly currency is not shared by the priest who encourages them to cultivate these virtues. Although he too seeks revenge, he expects to be paid in the all-too-human currency of secular power. Here we should note that Nietzsche faults neither the 'weak people' nor the priest for wishing to be paid for their virtue. As we shall see in our consideration of Essay II, the expression of this wish is perfectly natural for an animal bred within the system of incentives that drives the creditor–debtor relationship. What concerns him here is the cost to all parties of the self-hatred that is involved in pretending to cultivate virtue as its own reward.

Nietzsche thus raises the questions of *why* they must be compensated for their virtue, and *how*, but he postpones his answers to these questions until Essay II. In support of his claim that Christians need to be compensated for their virtue, he cites two venerable authorities, Thomas Aquinas (*c*.1225–74) and Tertullian (*c*.155–*c*.230), who confirm – the latter in vivid detail – that the arrival of the Kingdom of God will permit the weak and bedraggled to take delight in the eternal suffering of their erstwhile oppressors.[27] Especially in light of Nietzsche's avowed allegiance to 'Rome', it is worth noting that he does not translate these teachings of revenge into his native German, but allows them to stand in their original Latin. Having refused thus far to speak for Christianity, he thus allows Christianity to speak for itself, in the appropriated language of the Empire.

Section 16

Nietzsche concludes Essay I by proposing that the 'fearful struggle' between these 'two *opposing* values' (or value-systems) is chiefly responsible for determining the course of European civilization over the past two millennia. In an important qualification of this proposal, he allows that this struggle

has risen ever higher and thus become more and more profound and spiritual: so that today there is no more decisive mark of a '*higher nature*,' a more spiritual nature, than that of being divided in this sense [viz. self-divided] and a genuine battleground of these opposed values.[28]

It would be difficult to overestimate the importance of this qualification for Nietzsche's project in GM. First of all, he suggests that the literal battleground between nobles and slaves – if it ever existed as such – has long since been replaced by an internalized, spiritualized conflict. Within each of us, noble and servile impulses contest for dominance and preponderance.[29] Second, the future of humankind apparently depends upon the possibility of cultivating an ever-increasing *spiritualization* of the 'struggle' that each of us now hosts. As we shall see, in fact, the promise of a new, post-ascetic species of philosopher is directly related to the emancipation of the *spirit* that 'maternal' philosophers have secretly cultivated while masquerading as ascetic priests (GM III: 10). Finally, this spiritualized conflict continues to rage even today, in an epoch largely devoid of the material conditions of aristocracy. This means that Nietzsche and his readers may credibly aspire to create within themselves the *pathos* of distance that is uniquely emblematic of nobility.[30]

To those who still cannot see this struggle in its millennial protraction (cf. Section 8), Nietzsche recommends the following 'symbol': *Rome against Judea, Judea against Rome*. This easy-to-read symbol allows his readers to reduce the whole of European history in the Common Era to the struggle between opposing values (or value-systems). Having been named, that is, *Rome* and *Judea* acquire significance for even the least discerning of Nietzsche's readers. As he proceeds to explain, the ideals and active forces of 'Rome' have been exemplified, in succession, by the Roman Empire, the Renaissance, the counter-reformation, the *ancien régime* in France, and Napoleon; while the ideals and reactive forces of 'Judea' have been furthered by Christianity, the Reformation, the French Revolution and its aftermath. Borrowing from Nietzsche's analysis in Essay II, we might think of 'Rome' as representing the active forces that assert the primacy of the will to power, and of 'Judea' as representing the reactive forces that express the primacy of the will to existence. The will to power expresses itself by sacrificing the 'mass' to the possibility of the emergence of exotic singularities, while the will to existence preserves the 'mass' at the expense of the singularities that otherwise might arise (GM II: 12).

Of course, this symbol also may persuade some of Nietzsche's readers to entrench themselves ever more firmly in their pro-Roman or anti-Semitic sympathies,[31] which in turn may divert their focus from the amoral struggle that has determined the course of European civilization. This symbol is sufficiently simplistic, moreover, as to suggest a significant departure from Nietzsche's programme of education in GM. After training his readers to accustom themselves to subtle shades of variation, wispy traces of non-oppositional difference, and the depthless grey of the historical record, he now urges them to open their eyes to a graffito 'inscribed in letters legible across all human history'. That his description of this symbol evokes the pedagogical approach of the apostle Paul,[32] whom he despised, suggests that he may intend to waylay those readers who are unlikely to muster any greater degree of subtlety and sophistication than the proffered symbol requires. For these readers, his opening instructions – 'Let us conclude' – may refer not only to Essay I, but also to the programme of education in which they have been provisionally enrolled.

At the same time, however, the particular *content* of this symbol may serve to mitigate the partisanship it appears to encourage. First of all, the symmetry expressed by this symbol indicates that the opposing values (or value-systems) in question were equally responsible for, and indispensable to, the struggle that has ensued. The slave revolt in morality may have originated with the priestly Jews of Judea, but it did so only at the instigation of the Roman imperial presence. While the Jews had been oppressed and even enslaved before, they were provoked to the creative *ressentiment* of the slave revolt only by the influence of 'Rome' in the first century of the Common Era. The symmetry expressed by this symbol thus troubles any attempt to designate heroes and villains, winners and losers.

Nietzsche's choice of representative authorities furthermore reveals that this 'deadly contradiction' was rooted in a mutual misunderstanding, which both contestants were apparently powerless to resist. Just as 'Rome' – represented here by the historian Tacitus[33] – was wrong about the Jews, so was 'Judea' – represented here by St John – mistaken about the Roman Empire and the nations it incorporated. As the testimony of these dubious authorities confirms, neither contestant was in the right in any conventional sense. In fact, the content of this symbol serves to turn our attention toward their world-historical *pairing* in the struggle in which they were (and are) engaged. To pull for either contestant to secure a permanent victory over the other would be to assert the wish that the struggle – and, so, civilization itself – would come to an end.

Section 17

'Was that the end of it?' Nietzsche's sketch of Napoleon in the previous section suggests that it was not. The current crisis of European decadence, he implies, is a predictable reaction to the appearance of Napoleon, who burst upon the scene as an unanticipated, unthinkable monstrosity. As 'a last signpost to the *other* path', moreover, his appearance confirms that the noble lineage is still viable, its 'ancient fire' still smouldering.

Inasmuch as Napoleon represents the most recent resurgence of the active forces emblematic of 'Rome', we apparently are meant to understand that the reactive forces emblematic of 'Judea' are primarily concerned to *prevent* the 'synthesis of the *inhuman* and *superhuman*' that Napoleon came to embody. In other words, 'Judea' is now synonymous with the normalizing, constraining forces of culture itself. Precisely as Nietzsche feared, that is, 'the *meaning of all culture*' is now found in 'the reduction of the "human" beast of prey to a . . . *domestic animal*' (GM I: 11).

As we are now in a position to understand, however, the amoral rhythm of the struggle that defines European civilization eventually will favour once again the active forces of 'Rome'. As the reactive forces of 'Judea' exhaust themselves in the campaign to prevent another recurrence of the monstrous 'synthesis' embodied by Napoleon, culture itself will collapse and an indeterminate period of decadence will ensue. As the active forces of 'Rome' gain the upper hand in this struggle, the feared synthesis will become possible once again. Like all expressions of the primacy of active forces, the next instalment of 'Rome' will be glorious and all-too-brief, to be followed by another long period of decline. Such is the rhythm of this struggle.

Nietzsche's brief sketch of Napoleon thus suggests that the current crisis of European decadence is likely to beget an antipodal figure of unprecedented stature and form-giving power, someone who stands in relation to us as Napoleon stood to his contemporaries. As Nietzsche's rhetorical questions imply, in fact, the anticipated resurgence of 'Rome' *must* occur, as a matter of necessity. He consequently urges his readers to attach to this eventuality their most fervent 'desire' and 'will'. They need not aspire to *cause* this

ancient flame to 'flare up much more terribly', for its next con-
flagration is already in the works. They need simply will it to be so,
which means, as we shall see, that they must will the final collapse of
Christian morality (GM III: 27).

Nietzsche concludes Essay I with a 'note' in which he recommends a 'series of academic prize-essays', which would 'advance
historical studies of *morality*'. He even suggests a question to which
interested authors might respond, though it must be said that Essay
I of GM would be a presumptive favourite for the prize he has in
mind:

> '*What light does linguistics, and especially the study of etymology,
> throw on the history of the evolution of moral concepts?*'

Anticipating his later, triumphant incarnation as a *physiologist*, he
calls for a '*physiological* investigation and interpretation' of 'every
table of values'. Finally, he recommends the general reorganization of
all scholarly research around the pursuit of 'the solution to the
problem of value, the determination of the *order of rank among values*'.
As we shall see, he reserves for himself and his unknown 'friends' the
task of calling into question the value of truth itself (GM III: 24).

Summary

Nietzsche's alternative derivation of the concept of *good* is meant to
disclose the historical presence and operation of the noble morality,
to which the slave morality arose in reaction and response. The basic
value judgements of the noble morality are predicated on the distinction between *good* and *bad*, while the basic value judgements of
the slave morality are predicated on the opposition between *good*
and *evil*.

Nietzsche's juxtaposition of these two moralities is meant to
establish that the priority attached by contemporary morality to
the values associated with altruism is therefore contingent (rather
than necessary), relative (rather than absolute), acquired (rather than
natural), historical (rather than given) and context-dependent
(rather than context-independent). He concludes Essay I by proposing that the course of European civilization throughout the
Common Era has been determined by the ongoing struggle between
the value-systems associated respectively with these two moralities.
Although the current victory of the slave morality is undeniable, the

alternating rhythm of Western history buoys his hopes for a future graced by the resurgence of noble values.

Study questions

1. How does Nietzsche explain the origin of the concept of *good*?
2. What does Nietzsche mean by the 'slave revolt in morality'?
3. What is *ressentiment*, and what are its characteristic effects and expressions?
4. In what salient respects does the *noble morality* differ from the *slave morality*?
5. For what struggle does Nietzsche propose the symbol 'Rome against Judea, Judea against Rome'?

ESSAY II: 'GUILT', 'BAD CONSCIENCE' AND THE LIKE

Section 1

Essay II begins with a provocative pair of rhetorical questions:

> To breed an animal that *is permitted to make promises*[34] – is this not the paradoxical task that nature has set itself in the case of humankind? Is that not the real problem *regarding* humankind?

The first question announces Nietzsche's intention to treat human beings as they are treated, supposedly, by nature itself – namely, as animals in need of breeding. In developing his account of the origins of moral responsibility, he thus attempts to rely exclusively on the naturalistic principles of animal–human psychology. This question furthermore attests to his focus in Essay II on the convergence of nature's task with the distinctly moral project of producing animals that *are permitted* to promise. That nature has taken up this task, the second question suggests, is the source of the 'problem' that humankind both encounters and has become. Taking seriously this task may help us to understand why the future of humankind remains problematic.

Nietzsche's recourse here to rhetorical questions also affords him a measure of critical distance from the anthropomorphisms that his reference to nature's task would seem to imply. While he regards nature as task-oriented with respect to the evolution of the human species, the breeding process he describes is not predicated on any familiar model of human (i.e. cognitive, goal-directed) design.

Although nature has thus far selected the human animal for survival, it has not done so on the basis of any pre-ordained plan that exempts the human species from the threat of extinction.[35] As we shall see, in fact, he arrives at his determination of nature's task only by considering the long series of contingent, unforeseen developments through which humankind has become what it is. While in no conventional sense the *telos* of natural selection, the breeding of an animal that is permitted to promise would be consistent with the evolution thus far of the human species.

This task is *paradoxical*, as we shall see, because nature's breeding project must accommodate two developments that would appear to count as un- or anti-natural. The first of these developments, which occurred in the dim prehistory of the species (see Sections 16–18), resulted in the estrangement of the human animal from its native instincts. Prior to this development, Nietzsche conjectures, the human animal relied on its instincts for the automatic regulation of its most basic organic functions. Once estranged from its instincts, the human animal was obliged under the threat of extinction to acquire a memory, so that it would not forget the basic principles and precepts that would govern its efforts at self-regulation. In the case of human beings, that is, nature's task is to breed an animal equipped with a fully functional memory for the promises on which its post-instinctual survival depends.

Why, then, does Nietzsche present this task as unfinished and ongoing? Virtually everyone is (or feels) entitled to make promises, and the practice of promise-keeping is widely regarded as a cornerstone of contemporary morality. This brings us to the second of the two apparently anti-natural developments in the evolution of the human animal. In order to survive its post-instinctual existence, the human animal contracted the illness of the bad conscience, which in turn rendered it susceptible to the Christian teaching of guilt. Owing to the influence of Christian morality, the human animal now labours under the crushing burden of a guilty conscience. Having earned the prerogative to stand security for its future, the human animal now finds itself lacking a will for its future. In the process of becoming responsible for its promises, the human animal has become irresponsible to and for *itself*.

In order to prepare his readers to appreciate why this task remains as yet unfinished, Nietzsche reminds them of the powerful, countervailing force with which memory must contend: *forgetting*. With respect to the instinctual regulation of an animal organism, forget-ting is both more natural and more efficient than remembering. Far from an inertial force or defect, forgetting is in fact an 'active' force, which facilitates the process of 'inpsychation' (or psychological digestion) by allowing individuals to bypass consciousness as they absorb new experiences. By preserving the 'psychic order', the active force of forgetting thus contributes to the '*robust* health' of those animals in which it operates at full strength.

As this last point indicates, Nietzsche regards the acquisition of memory as necessarily involving the human animal in a departure from the health it formerly and naturally enjoyed. He consistently treats the investiture of memory not only as a physiological trauma in its own right, but also as a compensatory response to the more basic illness associated with the inwardly directed discharge of animal aggression (GM II: 16). On the one hand, then, he presents the acquisition of memory as both remarkable and improbable, especially in light of the enormous expenditure of energy that is needed simply to suspend the countervailing force of forgetting.[36] On the other hand, he presents the acquisition of memory as absolutely essential to the survival of the human animal in its post-instinctual existence. Under the threat of extinction, the human animal managed to withstand the suffering involved in acquiring an 'opposing faculty, a memory', on which it could rely to suspend the active force of forgetting.

Section 2

Here Nietzsche reveals that the task identified in the previous section – namely, that of breeding an animal permitted to promise – actually presupposes the 'preparatory task' of making human beings 'to a certain degree necessary, uniform, like among like, regular, and con-sequently calculable'. In order to become responsible for their oblig-ations, primitive human beings first needed to acquire the ability to relate to themselves in such a way that they could credibly assess their capacity to honour a particular promise or pledge. In turning now to consider this preparatory task, he announces his intention to trace our contemporary notion of moral responsibility to its origins in the pre-moral, pre-historical development of the human animal. He thus signals that his earlier account of responsibility (see GM I: 13) applies only to a relatively recent development, the history and pre-history of which he now aims to reconstruct.

The preparatory task of making human beings calculable was carried out and completed in the prehistory of the human species, prior to the convergence of nature's task with the civilizing project of morality. Here Nietzsche refers to the *morality of mores*, which his earlier writings identify as a form of ethical life that honours the norms embedded in custom and tradition as the only valid standards for human behaviour. Unlike our contemporary morality, which places a premium on individual responsibility and reflective deliberation, the morality of mores emphasized collective responsibility and uncritical, categorical adherence to established customs and traditional practices.[37] Under the aegis of the morality of mores, Nietzsche explains, primitive human beings were fashioned into future-oriented creatures, invested with a memory for their implicit promises to uphold the traditions to which they had become accustomed. Having become calculable in their own right, primitive human beings thus acquired the ability to calculate with respect to their collective future.

The meaning and justification of this 'tremendous process' became apparent only at its end, when the morality of mores unexpectedly produced individuals who, in brazen defiance of the customs and traditions that defined their collective existence, resolved to 'stand security for [*their*] *own future*' (GM II: 1). The measures employed to create a docile collective of promise-making animals actually empowered some of these animals to liberate themselves, *qua* individuals, from the customs and traditions of the collective. Eventually, that is, the morality of mores presided over the production of its *other*, i.e. that which it most strictly proscribed and forbade.[38] The 'ripest' of these fruits is the *sovereign individual*, whose unexpected emergence confirms the power of nature to elicit an exalted experience of 'self-mastery' from conditions of enforced uniformity. No longer 'like among like', i.e. an anonymous, interchangeable member of the collective, the sovereign individual is 'like only to himself', i.e. endowed by the morality of mores with a personal sense of obligation and responsibility. Liberated from the morality of mores, the sovereign individual is 'autonomous and supramoral',[39] which means that he appeals to something other than custom and tradition – something unique and idiosyncratic to himself – to guide his life. The sovereign individual thus considers himself justified in weighing the wisdom of tradition and determining for himself which of the prevailing customs he will and will not observe. He grants *himself* the permission he needs, having been bred by nature to do so.

What is most unique about the sovereign individual is that his self-awareness and self-consciousness have 'penetrated to the profoundest depths and become instinct, the dominating instinct'. This means that the morality of mores, which was meant to ensure that only custom and tradition would 'become instinct' in human animals, actually furnished some of the animals with a dominating instinct that could operate independently of custom and tradition. The sovereign individual is thus said to possess

> a proud consciousness, quivering in every muscle, of what has at length been achieved and become flesh in him, a . . . sensation of humankind come to completion.

If asked to name his dominating instinct, moreover, he would no doubt call it his *conscience*, by which he would mean to identify the inner voice that guides him. He is permitted to make promises, that is, on the strength of his conscience, which allows him to experience his emerging sense of individual responsibility not as a burden, but as a 'privilege'. The fruition of the sovereign individual thus marked the first, provisional completion of nature's task.

To be sure, the sovereign individual resembles in certain respects the nobles described in Essay I.[40] He possesses, and forms his evaluations on the basis of, the *pathos* of distance that is characteristic of the noble mode of valuation. Witness, for example, his sense of 'superiority' over others and his awareness of the 'trust', 'fear' and 'reverence' he inspires in them. Like the nobles, moreover, he 'possesses his [own] *measure of value*', which means that he is not reliant on others for his defining sense of identity and purpose. His estimations of himself and others furthermore call to mind the crude simplicity of the noble mode of valuation. Like the nobles, he divides the social world into those who are like him, e.g. the 'strong and reliable', and those who are not, e.g. the feckless 'windbags' and 'liars' who earn his scorn. Finally, his sense of his permission to make promises, which authorizes acts of violence toward those who are not similarly entitled, recalls the basis on which the Greek nobles were said to distinguish themselves, as 'the truthful', from the 'lying common man' (GM I: 5). In this light, we may think of the sovereign individual as the pre-historic progenitor of the nobles described in Essay I.[41]

Section 3

Nietzsche immediately acknowledges how odd it must sound to his readers that the sovereign individual would associate his achievement of self-mastery with his *conscience*. After all, his readers might respond, isn't a conscience precisely what is lacking in the sovereign individual?

As this retort attests, Nietzsche's readers are far more likely to regard the call of conscience as an impediment to the achievement of self-mastery. The typical experience of conscience, he realizes, is that of a hectoring, punitive monitor, which displays a cruel sense of timing as it reminds us of our faults and failings. Just as we begin to resemble the sovereign individual – e.g. feeling good about ourselves and superior to others, taking pride in our accomplishments, celebrating our independence and self-reliance, envisioning a future that would reflect our will, formulating promises that are both daring and meaningful, and so on – the conscience intrudes, poisoning our bliss and deflating our hopes for the future.

Nietzsche's rhetorical aim here is to reveal the extent to which his readers uncritically rely on a particular interpretation of conscience – namely, the *bad conscience* – which has only recently become authoritative. Prior to the moral period of human history, he asserts, an alternative interpretation of conscience was both possible and preferred. As the example of the sovereign individual is meant to demonstrate, the emphasis of this alternative interpretation is placed not on the potentially debilitating sting of conscience, but on the impetus to self-mastery that a robust conscience provides. So although it may be tempting to dismiss the sovereign individual as a primitive sociopath, we are urged here to consider the possibility that he too is a creature of conscience. His possession of a *good* (or *innocent*) conscience, which furnishes him with guidance and permission, is meant to illustrate that the *bad conscience* is neither the only, nor the best, interpretation available to us of the (admittedly painful) experience of internal duality that marks us as civilized beings. That one interprets this experience as evidence of one's unpaid debts – or, in the case of Christian morality, as evidence of one's faulted being – is simply a reflection of one's situation within the moral period of human development. Even within this period, moreover, the constructive role of conscience remains both underexplored and underreported.

This is not to suggest, of course, that we may return to the innocent conscience of the sovereign individual, or that Nietzsche urges us to do so. If the human animal is to survive the moral period of its development, it must do so in spite of – or, ideally, owing to – the burden of its bad conscience. As we shall see, Nietzsche speculates that the corrosive power of the bad conscience may yet be turned against the anti-affective second nature that we have acquired under the civilizing regime of culture (GM II: 24). In that event, the bad conscience may yet serve as the basis for a new, evolved claim to self-mastery.

Having previewed the end of this 'tremendous process', at which point the sovereign individual steps forth as a liberated creature of conscience, Nietzsche returns to his explanation of the process itself. In particular, he resumes his account of the acquisition of memory. His allusion to the human animal in its pre-memorial incarnation – 'attuned only to the passing moment' – indicates that he intends to treat memory as an emergent, compensatory organ. In support of his naturalistic account of the origins of responsibility, that is, he aims to provide a naturalistic account of the acquisition and expansion of memory.

The key to this latter account is the unusually strong emphasis he places on the use of *trauma* to endow these pre-memorial creatures with a functioning memory. Here Nietzsche does not mince words: the human animal acquired its memory through the application of the most brutal, painful and invasive techniques imaginable. As this account suggests, trauma is indispensable to the formation and expansion of memory. While this does not mean that human beings remember only what is seared into their flesh, it does mean that memories of a more singular, joyous nature are readily displaced by memories escorted into consciousness by trauma. Along with the lesson or prohibition to be memorialized, of course, one also tends to remember the trauma itself, which means that at some level of somatic experience, one is obliged to relive the founding trauma.

As Nietzsche explains later on (see Section 17), these techniques were developed and applied in the service of an ambitious campaign to domesticate (and subsequently exploit) those primitive human beings whose violent capture marked the founding of the earliest forms of human society. In exchange for their share in the benefits of civil society, these captives pledged to adhere faithfully to the customs and traditions of the collective. In order for their pledge to be meaningful, however, they first needed to acquire a memory for their promises. Subjected to a diet of physical suffering that was sufficiently intense as to penetrate *inward*, these captives contracted a previously unknown expanse of interiority, in which they could keep and revisit the promises extracted from them. From this point forward, they were reminded from without and from within of the customs of the society, which they were expected to observe without question or exception. The community in turn acquired a collective, public identity of its own, which it maintained on the strength of its credible threat to renew the founding trauma. The practice of what we now know as *punishment* thus began as an attempt to tame those primitive human beings who were forcibly immured in the earliest communities.

So it was that primitive human beings were made responsible for their adherence to the customs and traditions that sustained them in their collective, social existence. What we have yet to learn, of course, is how some of these human beings also managed to become responsible for *themselves*, such that they were permitted to make promises independent of the demands of custom and tradition.

Section 4

Having offered a preliminary account of the origins of responsibility, Nietzsche now poses the central question of Essay II: What is the origin of the 'bad conscience'? That is, how did the call of conscience come to be exclusively interpreted as a nagging reminder of one's faults and failings? Contrary to what the previous section may have led us to conclude, he does not wish to attribute the emergence of the bad conscience to the primitive techniques described in the previous section. In fact, his nostalgia for the good old days of flesh-searing mnemotechnics is a product of his conviction that the prehistoric practice of punishment actually served to postpone 'the development of the feeling of guilt' (GM II: 14).

Before he can answer this central question, however, he first must expose and discredit the misinterpretations that have been disseminated by his 'worthless' rivals. According to Nietzsche, his rivals err in placing a concept of relatively recent emergence – namely, moral guilt, which presupposes freedom of the will and the intention to cause harm – at the very origin of the practice of punishment. According to them, responsibility has always been a *moral* concept, for it has always been assigned on the basis of what one is and is not free to do. It thus follows, or so they insist, that punishment has always been dispensed only to those who are morally guilty, i.e. those who could and should have acted differently.

Nietzsche contends, however, that the assignment of responsibility on the basis of free will is itself a cultural achievement, which was thousands of years in the making. Before human beings were in a position to acquire a sense of personal responsibility, they first needed to become the kinds of creatures to whom personhood (or individuality) could be meaningfully attributed. To make his point, he once again plays the trump card of etymology:

> the major moral concept *guilt* [*Schuld*] has its origin in the very material concept *debts* [*Schulden*].

This hypothesis would seem to involve an application (or perhaps an adaptation) of the *rule of conceptual transformation*, which he advanced, also in response to the errors of his rivals, in Essay I. In both cases, a moral concept is traced back to its origins in a distinctly pre-moral concept, which reflects the material and political conditions of an earlier situation.[42] In both cases, moreover, an attention to etymology reveals the vestige of an earlier convention within a later convention, which explodes any claim that the later convention is either natural or given. So it is, he maintains, that the feeling of guilt, which we commonly associate with the 'sting' of conscience, can be traced to the material reality of being indebted to – and punished by – one's creditors. He thus proposes to centre the 'long story of how *responsibility* originated' on the transformation of the (pre-moral) concept of *debt* into the (moral) concept of *guilt*.[43]

This means, of course, that punishment could not have originated as a practice targeting offenders who were known to be morally guilty. As Nietzsche aims to demonstrate, in fact, punishment has been integral to the production of individuals who could be condemned as guilty agents. In stark contrast to his rivals, he thus declares that

> punishment, as requital, evolved quite independently of any presupposition concerning freedom or non-freedom of the will.

Having already speculated on the unflattering origins of this presupposition (GM I: 13), he now reaches back into the dim prehistory of the human animal, wherein punishment served as a means of expressing anger at some harm or injury, vented on the one who caused it – but this anger is held in check and modified by the idea that every injury has its *equivalent* and can actually be paid back, even if only through the *pain* of the culprit.

The idea of this equivalency 'drew its power', he now reveals, from the 'contractual relationship between *creditor* and *debtor*', which 'in turn points back to the fundamental forms of buying, selling, barter, trade, and traffic'.[44] In order to disclose the origins of guilt and responsibility, that is, he first must account for the notion of *indebtedness* that informed the earliest contractual relationships. In doing so, moreover, he must prepare his uunsuspecting readers to receive his alternative account of the origin of the bad conscience.

In the sections to follow, he appeals to the formative power of the creditor–debtor relationship to describe three distinct stages in the development of the concepts of *responsibility* and *obligation*. The first stage describes the emergence of *legal* obligations (Sections 5–10). The development of individual contracts is treated in Sections 5–8, and the development of civil law is treated in Sections 9–10. The second stage describes the emergence of *religious* obligations (Sections 19–20), and the third stage describes the emergence of *moral* obligations (Sections 21–22). A possible fourth stage of development, in which an as-yet-unformed concept of *extra-moral* responsibility might emerge, is sketched in Section 24.

In charting these stages of development, Nietzsche hopes to demonstrate that the human animal has strayed perilously far from its pursuit of a functional (i.e. species-preserving) sense of personal responsibility. Having earned the prerogative to stand security for its future, the human animal once again finds itself facing an uncertain future. This is why Nietzsche regards nature's 'breeding' project as ongoing, despite its initial completion, thousands of years ago, in the fruition of the sovereign individual.

Section 5

Placing the creditor–debtor relationship within the larger context of nature's breeding project, Nietzsche asserts that the earliest contracts furnished bloodthirsty creditors with a pretence and justification for the cruelty they desired in any event to visit upon their inferiors. Far from fair agreements made in good faith between mutually respectful parties of equal standing, the earliest contracts entitled bloodthirsty creditors to extract promises of repayment from hapless, pre-memorial debtors, whom they knew (or suspected) would not keep their promises. In exchange for a (barely) tolerable delay in the gratification of their instinct for cruelty, these creditors were assured the support of the entire community in the (likely) event that their debtors were to default. When the community finally allowed these disappointed creditors to vent their pent-up animal aggression, it did so under the emerging aspect of *legal punishment*.

According to Nietzsche, the gratuitous cruelty licenced by these earliest contracts proved to be indispensable to the success of nature's campaign to breed individuals who were responsible for their promises.[45] By virtue of this arrangement, creditors grew accustomed to the attachment of conditions to their enjoyment of cruelty, while debtors were granted an opportunity-cum-incentive to improve their memories. Unbeknownst to these creditors, in fact, the cruelty they legally enjoyed had the effect over time of equipping their debtors with a reliable memory for their promises. As debtors became progressively more heedful, especially as punishment became increasingly codified and institutionalized, they also became more responsible. Over time, as Shylock ruefully discovered, the pure pleasure involved in visiting cruelty upon defaulted debtors grew ever more elusive.

This hypothesis is supported, Nietzsche insists, by the otherwise inexplicable preoccupation, on the part of those who authored the earliest known laws and contracts, with the details of corporal punishment. While various forms of collateral could be offered as security, the debtor ultimately was obliged to pledge his own person, his flesh-and-blood body, in compensation for his likely failure to provide adequate and timely repayment. The promise of corporal punishment thus established an equivalency between the debtor's injury to the creditor and the pleasure the creditor may take in 'being allowed to vent his power freely upon one who is powerless'. This particular form of compensation furthermore allowed the injured creditor to participate in an ancient '*right of the masters*', which entitled him to treat others as if they were 'beneath him'. As we shall see, Nietzsche's appeal here to a natural instinct for cruelty is also meant to establish a natural basis for the earliest forms of morality, law, politics and religion.

The pleasure to be derived from cruelty is simply and exclusively gratuitous.[46] For this reason, in fact, it is directly related to the social distance that separates the creditor from the debtor. The less significant the debtor, the greater the pleasure the creditor may derive from inflicting cruelty upon him. If Nietzsche is right about the general collapse of the order of rank in late modernity, we should not be surprised to discover that we have no direct or uncomplicated experience of this kind of pleasure. Inasmuch as we regard everyone else as roughly equal to ourselves, we cannot know the pure, gratuitous pleasure described in this section. This does not mean, of course, that we do not treat others as if they were beneath us; it simply means that we do not enjoy our mistreatment of them with a good conscience.

So it was, Nietzsche believes, that nature harnessed the cruelty of primitive human beings to advance its project of breeding a responsible animal. Within the formative context of the creditor–debtor relationship, the natural instinct for cruelty was trained to become indirectly productive of memory, which in turn allowed some debtors to avoid (or mitigate) the punishment for which they were contractually liable. In light of this explanation, we should not be surprised to learn that human beings expect to be *paid* for their cultivation of virtue, and that they prefer to be compensated in the suffering and blood of their enemies. As we shall see, in fact, Nietzsche is determined to show that morality too derives its purchase from its promise to pay its adherents for their cultivation of virtue.

Section 6

Here Nietzsche introduces the moral concepts he means to explain in Essay II, tracing the origin of 'their moral conceptual world' to the primitive 'sphere of legal obligations' that he has just described. As he earlier surmised, that is, the contemporary moral notion of *personal obligation* (or *guilt*) originated in the primitive, pre-moral relationship between creditors and debtors.

Before he proceeds any further, however, he acknowledges how barbaric it must sound to us that 'suffering can balance debts or guilt'. In particular, he concedes that it will be difficult for anyone today, including himself and his best readers, to attain a

> really vivid comprehension of the degree to which *cruelty* constituted the great festival pleasure of more primitive humans.

His rhetorical aim here is to encourage his readers to acknowledge (and explore) their own enjoyment of cruelty. Towards this end, he forwards two observations. First of all, 'higher culture' does not abolish cruelty, but pursues (and sponsors) it in increasingly 'spiritualized' forms. So although we may recoil from gory displays of corporal violence, we may delight in more sublime expressions of cruelty. Second, we moderns are not so refined as to be entirely unfamiliar with the primitive enjoyment of overt displays of gratuitous cruelty. Indeed, the narrative of Essay II would make little sense if Nietzsche could not identify the familial continuity – however faint, sublimated, repressed or criminalized it may be – that connects the experiences of his delicate contemporaries with those of the primitive, bloodthirsty humans described in this section. Having identified the natural instinct for cruelty that characterizes the human animal in all of its incarnations thus far, he may very well expect the best of his civilized readers to smile knowingly as he illustrates the festive quality of these supposedly primitive rituals of punishment.

Section 7

In what amounts to an exhortatory interlude, Nietzsche insists that making others suffer has served in the past, and may yet serve in the future, as a seduction to life. The future of humankind is imperilled neither by cruelty nor by its enjoyment, he explains, but by 'the increase in humankind's feeling of shame *at humankind*'.

The contemporary campaign to abolish suffering is wrong-headed in many respects, but its signal failing is its misidentification of the real problem. 'What really arouses indignation against suffering,' he explains, 'is not suffering as such but the senselessness of suffering.' Human beings are actually adept at the art of justifying their otherwise meaningless suffering, whether by appealing to the Christian's 'mysterious machinery of salvation' or by virtue of the more ancient preoccupation with the 'spectator' or 'causer' of suffering. Previewing the main thesis of Essay III, he furthermore proposes that life itself is and always has been the author of our most successful responses to the suffering that marks our existence. In fact, he implies, a true optimist always should trust in life to devise new ways to seduce us to its charms.

In support of this claim, he appeals explicitly to ancient Greek mythology and moral philosophy, both of which made sense of human suffering by placing human beings *on stage*. In their festival plays (in the case of mythology) and tragedies (in the case of moral philosophy), the Greeks presented human suffering as a topic of unending interest and amusement to their gods. As we shall see, in fact, this interpretative approach allowed the ancient Greeks to refuse responsibility for their most heinous crimes (GM II: 23), including their gratuitous displays of 'festive' cruelty. (If these festivals are demanded by the gods, after all, then *our* enjoyment of the cruelty inflicted therein is both innocent and irrelevant.) That human beings now deem themselves unworthy (or only selectively worthy) of divine interest is a far greater calamity than the suffering produced by the natural instinct for cruelty.

Section 8

Nietzsche returns to his investigation by reviewing its progress thus far. He has traced the concept of moral responsibility to its origins in the notion of legal responsibility, which in turn took shape in the context of the primitive relationship between creditor and debtor. He turns now to describe the process of individuation through which a sense of *personal* (as opposed to *collective*) responsibility was able to develop. As we shall see, this process culminates in the Christian teaching of guilt, on the strength of which individuals hold themselves personally responsible for their faulted existence.

It was in the evolving context of the creditor–debtor relationship, he now elaborates, that primitive human beings learned to measure themselves against each other. Here too the prospect of enjoying (or avoiding) cruelty provided a palpable incentive for them to refine their negotiating skills. Prospective creditors and debtors were obliged not only to acquire a keener understanding of one another, but also to cultivate those habits of *self*-attention that eventually would yield a set of distinctly self-regarding relationships. As they became ever more closely acquainted with themselves and others as individuals, Nietzsche implies, they slowly dissolved the bonds of custom and tradition that had tied them to the community. This process of individuation in turn produced in them a nascent sense of personal responsibility, which developed independently of the sense of collective responsibility that had been instilled in them by the morality of mores.

Nietzsche thus speculates that 'human pride', including the 'feeling of superiority' over others, may have arisen as a result of the calculations and determinations that made up so much of the 'earliest thinking' of primitive human beings. This is an important speculation on his part, for it allows him to suggest that the creditor–debtor relationship furnished the context within which some human beings acquired the skills and resources that would enable them, eventually, to emancipate themselves from the customs and traditions that sustained the community. Having learned to measure themselves against other buyers and sellers, and having prevailed in these transactions, they eventually would aspire to possess their own measure of value and their own sense of responsibility. From the crucible of the creditor–debtor relationship, he thus implies, the sovereign individual eventually would emerge.

But we are getting ahead of ourselves. For now, Nietzsche is content to claim that the skills and tactics required for effective participation in contractual (i.e. promise-based) relationships eventually improved to the point that primitive human beings

> arrived at the great generalization, 'everything has its price; *all* things can be paid for.'

This generalization provided the conceptual basis for the articulation of the earliest, most rudimentary notion of legal responsibility. Buyers and sellers acquired certain rights and responsibilities, as determined and enforced by the best among them. While this does not mean that contracts were no longer rigged to favour the creditors, it does mean that creditors increasingly acknowledged the usefulness of public standards of fairness. Nietzsche thus claims to discover in this grand generalization 'the oldest and most naive moral canon of *justice*', which predates (and so informs) the more familiar manifestation of justice as a social virtue. From this point forward, the creditor–debtor relationship developed within the framework provided by an increasingly specific legal code.

Of course, the emergence of a moral canon of justice implies the activity of individuals who are willing and able to enforce its standards of fairness. As we shall see, Nietzsche thus insists that 'legal conditions can never be other than *exceptional* conditions', for they invariably involve 'a partial restriction of the will of life, which is bent upon power' (GM II: 11). In order to explain the appearance of a rudimentary notion of legal responsibility, that is, he thus posits the appearance of a band of exceptional individuals, who agree to endure a self-imposed restriction of their drive for power:

> Justice on this elementary level is the good will among parties of approximately equal power to come to terms with one another . . .

and to *compel* parties of lesser power to reach a settlement among themselves.

Whence this 'good will' to which Nietzsche attributes the earliest glimmer of justice on earth? We are perhaps meant to believe that the unprecedented 'understanding' reached by these exceptional individuals reflects the natural (if extraordinary) progression of their ability to measure themselves and others. Convinced that '*all* things can be paid for', they discovered that they could afford to pay now – in the form of a voluntary restriction of the drive for power – for benefits to be reaped in the future. That is, they realized that a tolerable delay in the gratification of their natural instinct for cruelty might yield a bonanza of compensatory benefits. According to this (admittedly speculative) line of interpretation, Nietzsche traces the origins of justice to the emergence of primitive human beings who have acquired the ability to calculate future outcomes and who possess the will to endure voluntary restrictions of their drive to power.[47]

Although Nietzsche offers very little insight into the nature and character of these original arbiters of justice, his account of their founding 'settlement' is apparently meant to put us in mind of the nobles described in Essay I. In the elementary canon of justice described here, for example, we may detect in germinal form the *pathos* of distance that is characteristic of the noble morality. The 'good will' that enables these first champions of justice to reach a mutually acceptable 'understanding' suggests a rudimentary expression of the noble mode of valuation, especially inasmuch as they are able to distinguish between those who are and those who are not like them. Indeed, we should not be surprised to learn that Nietzsche concludes the healthy version of this 'long story of responsibility' with a discussion of the nobles of Greek antiquity (GM II: 23).

Section 9

Translating this primitive 'moral canon of justice' into distinctly social terms, Nietzsche expands his earlier analysis to explain the relationship between the primitive community (i.e. the 'disappointed creditor') and its lawbreakers (i.e. defaulted 'debtors' who have attacked their 'creditor'). The development of punishment as a social practice thus reflects the assertion by the primitive community of its rights to compensation from its defaulted debtors. Although Nietzsche rejects any appeal to a 'social contract' to explain the founding of the state

(GM II: 17), he relies here on a contractual model to explain the evolving relationship of the community to its members.

In order to account for the implied transition from the concept of *debtor* to that of *lawbreaker*, Nietzsche proposes that the actual harm caused by the defaulted debtor is less significant than the symbolic harm involved in breaking his contract '*with the whole* [community]'. This means that the aggrieved community is not only entitled to compel repayment, but also obliged to remind the lawbreaker of the true value of communal life. The community accomplishes both objectives by remanding the lawbreaker to a condition of internal exile, which effectively returns him to 'the savage and outlaw state' from which the community had rescued him. Punishment thus appeared in these earliest communities as 'simply a copy . . . of the normal attitude toward a hated, disarmed, prostrated enemy'. Both the threat and the reality of internal exile would have been particularly effective in refining the lawbreaker's appreciation of his personal responsibility to the community as a whole.

Section 10

Continuing his account of the development of this ancient moral canon of justice, Nietzsche speculates that the growth of the community produces a qualitative change in its self-understanding. Eventually, he explains, the thriving community becomes so powerful that it 'ceases to take so seriously the individual's transgressions'. The basic creditor–debtor relationship still obtains, as does the ancient equivalency on which it rests, but the creditor in question is now strong enough to ignore or forgive the transgressions of its debtors. Rather than consign its lawbreakers to internal exile, the community now comes to their defence and mediates between them and the angry victims of their crimes.

If, as he proposes, the severity of the penal law is inversely related to the power of the community, then it stands to reason that

> a society might attain such a *consciousness of power* that it could allow itself the noblest luxury possible to it – letting those who harm it go *unpunished*.

By treating justice as an index of the aggrieved creditor's power and self-confidence, Nietzsche positions himself to chart the transformation of justice from its 'most ancient moral canon' into its noblest incarnation to date – namely, as *mercy*. As we shall see, this account of the self-cancellation of justice enables him to extend his analysis of the creditor–debtor relationship into the spheres of ancestor worship and religion. When he resumes this narrative in Section 19, he will identify the community's 'most powerful men', for whom 'mercy remains the privilege', as the models not only for its ancestors, but also for its gods.

Nietzsche's account of the evolution of justice thus affords him the opportunity to introduce a concept of central importance to his genealogy of morals: *self-cancellation*,[48] which is the process of immanent transformation that attends and facilitates qualitative amplifications of power. Thus far, he has described the growth of the community's power in terms of incremental, quantitative changes. Here, however, he claims to discern an amplification of power that issues in qualitative changes, such that the community in question outgrows its previous understanding of justice. The strength of the community is now evident in its indifference to, rather than its reprisal against, its various debtors and lawbreakers. This qualitative development may yield immediate political benefits for the community in question, especially if its rivals correctly interpret its mercy as an unprecedented show of strength. In that event, the community's overt display of mercy would function as a kind of self-imposed handicap, for it would signal to rival communities the losses they except to incur in any skirmish with the community in question.[49]

The self-cancellation of justice not only affords the thriving community 'the noblest luxury possible', but also foreshadows the terms of its eventual, inevitable decline. In becoming merciful, the community suspends its traditional approach to the punishment of lawbreakers. In doing so, the community also – and probably unwittingly – abandons its role in the ongoing education and training of its erstwhile debtors. This is a critical development in the evolution of the community, for, as Nietzsche explains later on, a robust apparatus of punishment actually serves to prevent 'the development of the feeling of guilt' in those who are punished (GM II: 14). So long as lawbreakers receive the punishments they deserve, which usually bear some resemblance to the crimes for which they are held responsible, they understand that there is nothing remarkable, much less objectionable, about the nature of their deeds. They are punished not as guilty agents, but simply as 'instigator[s] of harm' whose actions have disturbed the peace of the community (GM II: 14). Once the merciful community suspends its traditional practice of punishment, however, these lawbreakers are likely to grow increasingly unfamiliar with the disruptive deeds through which the community exercises its own power. Free to entertain the possibility that their deeds are objectionable as such, they would eventually come to regard themselves as guilty agents, and their deeds as sins.

Here we may infer the influence of the priests, who become increasingly powerful as the thriving community embraces mercy as its new standard of social justice. In releasing its lawbreakers from their internal exile, the newly merciful community does not grant them equal rights and privileges; nor does it abolish existing class divisions. If anything, the self-cancellation of justice serves to exacerbate the social division between creditors and debtors. The mercy displayed by the community in fact expresses the escalating *contempt* of its leaders for its pesky criminals, who, as 'parasites', are no longer deemed worthy of the respect and attention owed to genuine enemies. Enduring these despised 'parasites' has become a sign of the community's health and strength.

Once relegated to the lower orders of society, these former lawbreakers are placed under the care of the priests, to whom the leaders of the community have delegated the task of brokering the afore-mentioned 'settlement' among 'parties of lesser power' (GM II: 8). It falls to the priests, that is, to quell the *ressentiment* of the lower orders and to prevent these 'parasites' from despoiling the good conscience of the community's leaders (GM II: 11). From this point forward, the lower orders – comprising lawbreakers, debtors, parasites and slaves – would enjoy the constant companionship of the priest, who eventually would persuade them to regard themselves as guilty agents. In doing so, as we shall see, the priest would also manage to transform these lower orders into instruments of his revenge against the nobles.

Section 11

This section serves as a polemical interlude, in which Nietzsche rebuts the popular notion that justice originated in the sphere of *ressentiment*. Here he recalls the discovery, reported earlier by his unnamed respondent, that justice is simply a 'sanctified' euphemism for the long-awaited revenge of the weak and downtrodden (GM I: 14). While he does not dispute that agents of *ressentiment* have sullied the concept of justice, he cautions his readers not to confuse the current euphemism with the (noble) origins of justice. Reviewing the argument outlined in Sections 8–10, he insists that the 'entire administration of law . . . [and] the need for law' belong to the 'sphere . . . of the active, strong, spontaneous, aggressive'. The institution of law is thus meant not to ban the expression of aggressive forces, but to redirect and channel these forces toward the realization of productive ends that are otherwise unattainable.

Taking issue with the anti-Semitic agitator Eugen Dühring (1833–1901), Nietzsche associates the administration of justice with the efforts of

a stronger power seeking a means of putting an end to the senseless raging of *ressentiment* among the weaker powers that stand under it.[50]

Pace Dühring, he insists that designations of what is 'just' and 'unjust' presuppose the prior institution of law and are therefore meaningless outside this context. If considered 'from the highest biological standpoint', in fact, the establishment of law must always appear 'exceptional', inasmuch as 'legal conditions' always involve a 'partial restriction of the will of life'. Those who would create and enforce laws, that is, must be sufficiently strong to do so, which rules out the puny agents of *ressentiment*. Indeed, Nietzsche may mean to allude here to the leaders of the community described in Section 10, especially inasmuch as they are prompted by their newfound mercy to modify their approach to the administration of justice. As we shall see, the approach they select will have serious implications for the long-term future of their community.

Section 12
As in the previous section, Nietzsche draws attention here to his own polemical presence in the main narrative. He begins this section, too, with an abrupt, inelegant transition, and he once again interrupts himself so that he might expose the methodological errors committed by his rivals.

Here he inveighs against those genealogists who routinely presume to infer the *origin* of punishment from its current or apparent *purpose*. By exposing this confusion, which is popularly known as (or associated with) the *genetic fallacy*, he is able to demonstrate that the most basic error of his rivals, from which all other errors and specious conclusions arise, is their misinterpretation of the nature of life itself. If we separate the origin of punishment from its various purposes, he explains, we are in a position to appreciate the following general insight:

> [A]ll events in the organic world are a subduing, a *becoming master*, and all subduing and becoming master involves a fresh interpretation, an adaptation through which any previous 'meaning' and 'purpose' are necessarily obscured or even obliterated.

This explanation of 'events in the organic world' sets the stage for his articulation of his own, alternative account of evolution:

> The 'evolution' of a thing, a custom, an organ, is thus by no means its *progressus* toward a goal, even less a logical *progressus* by the shortest route and with the smallest expenditure of force – but a succession of more or less profound, more or less mutually independent processes of subduing, plus the resistances they encounter, the attempts at transformation for the purpose of defense and reaction, and the results of successful counteractions.

As this passage suggests, Nietzsche aims to stake out a middle ground between the naive anthropomorphisms of the Social Darwinists on the one hand, and the nihilistic enthusiasm for the 'absolute fortuitousness, even the mechanistic senselessness of all events', on the other hand. Against the latter position, he insists that evolution *does* admit of discernible progress; against the former position, he proposes an amoral, non-cognitive model of evolutionary progress.[51] Rival champions of natural selection, he thus implies, have been constrained by their reluctance to consider what 'an actual *progressus*' would invariably involve: the *death* of an organ or organism as it contributes to the production of ever '*greater* units of power'. An organism participates in natural selection, that is, not by seeking to preserve itself,[52] but by seeking to discharge its strength, even if doing so hastens its own demise. This is true as well of human beings, whom rival theorists are typically keen to exempt from the cold, exacting calculus of natural selection. In the case of human beings, Nietzsche offers, the sacrifice of 'humankind in the mass . . . to the prosperity of a single *stronger* species of human being' would in fact constitute 'an advance'.

In explicit reaction to the spread of the 'democratic idiosyncrasy', Nietzsche identifies the 'essence of life' as its *'will to power'*,[53] which he associates with the expression of 'spontaneous, aggressive, expansive, form-giving forces that give new interpretations and directions'. His appeal to this alternative hypothesis is meant to discredit Herbert Spencer's influential campaign to locate the essence of life in its 'ever more efficient adaptation to external conditions'. While it is certainly true that living beings are adaptive, they also, and more basically, assert themselves actively against the world, thereby shaping the external resistances to which they also respond and adapt. Spencer, who originated the phrase 'survival of the fittest' to describe the mechanism of natural selection,[54] is thus presented here as representative of the deleterious influence of the 'democratic idiosyncrasy'. Personally opposed to 'everything that dominates and wants to dominate', he misidentifies what it would really mean for an organism or species to assert its fitness for survival.

As we shall see, Nietzsche's introduction of the will to power is meant in part to prepare us for his 'hypothesis concerning the origin of the "bad conscience"', which he will finally unveil in Section 16. This daring hypothesis explains the emergence of the human animal on the basis of an unprecedented upsurge of active forces. As his analysis of Spencer suggests, moreover, only those who can resist the thrall of the 'democratic idiosyncrasy' will be in a position to take seriously this hypothesis.

Section 13
Returning to his discussion of punishment, Nietzsche recommends a distinction between that which is 'relatively *enduring*' (e.g. its 'procedure') and that which is *'fluid'* (e.g. its 'meaning' or 'purpose') in punishment. The latter element, he further proposes, is typically *'projected* and interpreted *into'* the former element.

Thus it is not the case, as rival genealogists maintain, that the procedure of punishment is devised to fit its purpose; rather, its purpose is revealed as its procedure is enacted. Inasmuch as purpose follows procedure, any particular enactment of punishment may stimulate a fresh interpretation of its purpose and meaning. This means, in short, that punishment itself was not designed for the purpose of punishing. As we shall see, Nietzsche hypothesizes that punishment originated in a particular expression of spontaneous, form-giving animal aggression, which he attributes to 'artists' who were indifferent (and perhaps oblivious) to the victims of their aggression (GM II: 17). To prove his point, he compiles a list of the various purposes that punishment has served, all within the same basic structure or procedure.

Section 14

He breaks off this ghastly recitation so that he might debunk the popular notion that 'punishment is supposed to possess the value of awakening the *feeling of guilt* in the guilty person'. Nothing could be further from the truth, he insists, and he employs the ensuing analysis as the pivot on which he returns his main narrative to the topic of guilt.

The 'sting' of conscience, he observes, is rare among those who actually have been punished. Anyone who endures the punitive wrath of the community is unlikely to regard his own instigations of harm as somehow exceptional, much less as warranting moral condemnation. Rather than induce a feeling of guilt, in fact, punishment more typically 'makes men hard and cold'. This can only mean that the feeling of guilt first arose in those *who were not punished*. Here it becomes clear, in fact, that Nietzsche understands the primitive practice of punishment to involve only those forms of cruelty that are exclusively addressed to the body. Although he will go on to discuss other, more diabolical forms of cruelty, these should not be confused with the archaic practice of corporal punishment.

Throughout the prehistoric period of human existence, he claims, the practice of corporal punishment actually served to *postpone* the development of the bad conscience – and, so, of the feeling of guilt. The disruptive deed was not condemned as such, for the judges and punishers performed similar deeds, ostensibly in the service of justice. Only the individual was condemned, and he was punished only as an 'instigator of harm', whose memory for his promises needed to be refreshed. So long as he was subjected to a steady diet of corporal punishment, in fact, the offending individual was unlikely to see himself as a guilty agent who deserved the punishment he received. Only when he is finally removed from this diet, as we shall see, does he find himself at risk for the existential crisis that his punishment thus far has postponed.

Section 15

In support of the proposal advanced in Section 14, Nietzsche turns here to Benedict de Spinoza (1632–77), whom he applauds for banishing 'good and evil to the realm of human imagination'. When the world is returned thereby to its natural state of innocence, Spinoza concluded, 'the sting of conscience' is reduced to, or replaced by, 'a sadness accompanied by the recollection of a past event that flouted all of our expectations'. This sadness, Nietzsche concurs, comprises the full extent of the 'inward pain' suffered by those primitive human beings who were punished for failing to fulfil their contractual obligations. As we have seen, no effort was made in prehistoric times to punish the deed as such, and the doer of the deed was punished only in order to encourage his 'prudence' in making and keeping promises. Sadly, this nugget of primitive wisdom has been misplaced by civilized champions of punishment, who claim (and apparently believe) that the 'taming' of human beings actually makes them 'better'.

Section 16

Having exposed and corrected the mistakes of his rivals, Nietzsche finally returns to the question he raised in Section 4: what is the origin of the 'bad conscience'? An answer to this question will help us to understand how, and why, nature's pursuit of its paradoxical task required the human animal to forfeit its access to the *good* (or *innocent*) conscience of the sovereign individual.

Here, as elsewhere in GM, form and content coincide. Nietzsche abruptly interrupts his own narrative to posit a sudden, unforeseen rupture in the development of the human animal. The urgency of this interruption is certainly understandable, for he has proceeded thus far on the assumption that the human animal could serve as an apt recipient of an implanted memory *and* as a credible bearer of personal responsibility. Having cultivated in his readers the 'second sight' that is missing in his rivals (GM II: 4), Nietzsche is now in a position to explain how the human animal could have become self-oriented and interiorized to the extent required by his account thus far. It did so, he conjectures, on the strength of a self-inflicted wound, which effectively removed human beings from the animal kingdom and deprived them of the instinctual regulation enjoyed by all other animals. The circumstances under which the human animal sustained and survived this self-inflicted wound are meant to explain how it initially acquired the minimal expanse of interiority that the creditor–debtor relationship both presupposes and develops.

As we soon discover, Nietzsche's hypothesis ranks among the most original and daring insights of his (and anyone's) philosophical career. No wonder it could wait no longer:

> I regard the bad conscience as the serious illness that humankind was bound to contract under the stress of the most fundamental change ever experienced – that change which occurred when human beings found themselves finally enclosed within the walls of society and peace.

This compact passage bundles together three related claims. First of all, Nietzsche posits a sudden, unanticipated rupture in the development of the human animal, which is supposed to explain its involuntary transition from an instinctual to a post-instinctual form of existence. Second, he wishes to account for this rupture in terms of the 'most fundamental change ever experienced' by the human animal – namely, its captivity within the gilded cage of civil society. Third, he wishes to trace the onset of the illness of the bad conscience to the unprecedented 'stress' involved in this change, which obliged the human animal to turn its unspent natural aggression against itself. He thus intends to trace the origin of responsibility to the improbable emergence of an animal divided *against itself*, an animal involuntarily estranged from its natural instincts.

Nietzsche's articulation of this hypothesis is complicated by his conflation of three distinct and potentially separable stages in the progression of this species-altering illness. In the first stage, the human animal was suddenly afflicted with the suffering that attends the mandatory introjection (or inward discharge) of its natural instincts. The inward discharge of instinctual aggression invested the human animal with an unprecedented experience of interiority, which allowed (and in fact required) it to develop those habits of self-attention and self-correction that eventually became constitutive of the familiar, self-regarding relationship in which human beings (especially *qua* moral agents) now stand.[55] At least initially, those members of the species that survived this transition regarded their self-inflicted suffering as nothing more than a misfortune that had unexpectedly befallen them, not unlike the suffering inflicted by a crashing boulder, a bolt of lightning, or a rampaging predator. That is, they did not yet suffer from the *meaning* of their suffering.

The first stage in the progression of this illness is thus marked by the emergence of the *conscience*, which Nietzsche understands as the experience of interiority (or internal duality) that invariably attends the inward discharge of one's instinctual aggression.[56] Although this experience subjected primitive humans to an unfamiliar regimen of self-inflicted suffering, it also encouraged them to cultivate these habits of self-attention that would enable (some of) them to attain an experience of self-mastery. If contracted by human beings who can accept this self-inflicted suffering as a non-negotiable condition of their post-instinctual existence, this illness need not advance beyond the first stage in its progression. As we shall see, in fact, Nietzsche presents the nobles of Greek antiquity as creatures of conscience who were able to 'ward off' the disease of the bad conscience (GM II: 23), even as this disease become pandemic among those whom they deemed as *bad*.

The second stage in the progression of this illness commenced when one of these caged animals, already tormented by the mandatory introjection of his native cruelty, *also* began to suffer 'from the problem of his meaning' (GM III: 28). He did so, as we are now in a position to understand, when the community mercifully suspended its traditional regimen of corporal punishment (GM II: 10). As a result, he thus began to suffer the 'inward pain' that the recently suspended programme of corporal punishment held to a minimum (GM II: 14). Unable to distract himself from his self-inflicted suffering, this caged animal began to regard his experience of inferiority (viz., his conscience) as an objection to his very existence. A full-blown existential crisis ensued. He needed to know why he suffered, and he needed to understand why he should continue to endure a life predicated on such suffering (GM III: 28). The door to 'suicidal nihilism' had been opened (GM III: 28).

The third stage in the progression of this illness is marked by the transformation of this tortured, miserable creature into 'the inventor of the "bad conscience"'.[57] On the advice of the ascetic priest, the caged animal sought the cause of his suffering 'in *himself*, in some *guilt*, in a piece of the past' (GM III: 20). Under the aegis of the ascetic ideal, he soon came to understand his suffering as a well-deserved punishment – not for being cruel to others, which he was prevented from doing, but for *wishing* to be cruel to others. He thus convinced himself that his suffering was the punishment he deserved for harbouring a natural instinct for cruelty. On the strength of this interpretation, the suffering that he was bound in any event to inflict upon himself became an acceptable, enjoyable – even *preferred* – alternative to the outward discharge of his instinctual cruelty. The third stage in the progression of this illness is thus marked by the determination of the conscience as *bad*, i.e. as a nagging reminder of the burden of those debts and misdeeds that may be attributed to one's untamed animal nature. In this third stage of the illness, sufferers gladly forfeit any possible recourse to their experience of interiority (or internal duality) as a resource potentially conducive to, or constitutive of, self-mastery. For these sufferers, the *good* conscience of the sovereign individual can be nothing more than a myth, a cruel joke on hapless humans, or a euphemistic diagnosis of the amoral sociopath.

In its fully developed form, the illness of the bad conscience thus involves three moments or layers of distress: 1) one suffers from the self-directed cruelty (i.e. conscience) that is required of all human beings under the civilizing regime of culture; 2) one suffers this self-directed cruelty to the point of triggering an existential crisis, which is sufficiently dire that it distracts from one's physical suffering; and 3) one suffers from the additional burden of the consciousness of one's indebtedness, which is sufficiently grave as to deflate (or postpone) the looming crisis. In its fully developed form, that is, the bad conscience manifests itself as a compound illness: Physical suffering gives rise to existential distress, which in turn makes one conscious of one's flaws and failings, for which one deserves to suffer. This realization enables one to interpret one's self-inflicted suffering as the dispensation of a just punishment, which targets one's untamed animal nature. As we shall see, this is the form of the illness that supports, and perhaps invites, the Christian interpretation of the bad conscience as evidence of one's *guilt*. As a guilty agent, or so the story goes, one deserves to receive an indeterminate punishment for one's irremediable faults and failings.

Perhaps the most interesting thing about the invention of the bad conscience is that it did not aim to heal – and in fact exacerbated – the condition of self-division that had befallen the human animal in its post-instinctual existence. At the urging of the priest, the inventor of the bad conscience cleverly interpreted his conscience – complete with the self-regarding relationship and habits of self-attention it had prompted him to cultivate – as the centrepiece of a newly fashioned sense of self, to which individual responsibilities and obligations could be meaningfully assigned. Now siding with consciousness, reason, and the other feeble organs of regulation on which he had become involuntarily reliant, this miserable creature issued 'a declaration of war against the old instincts', blaming them for the suffering he endured and targeting them with the aggression he was obliged in any event to vent against himself. The illness of the bad conscience thus provided him with a constant (and fixed) target for the discharge of his native cruelty – namely, himself, *qua* guilty repository of animal vitality. Despite burdening the human animal with an unwieldy, inefficient system of bodily regulation, the illness of the bad conscience positioned this troubled species to survive its involuntary estrangement from its natural instincts.

Having abruptly forwarded this daring 'hypothesis', Nietzsche now backtracks a bit and identifies the novel physiological-psychological theory on which it rests:

> All instincts that do not discharge themselves outwardly turn inward – this is what I call the *internalization* of the human animal.

Although he does not elaborate on this theory in any detail, he apparently means for us to accept the following claims: 1) human psychology is simply a complicated instance of animal psychology; 2) the basic processes of animal psychology are best understood as articulations of unconscious drives and instincts; 3) it would be possible for a species to survive, and adapt to, the enforced introjection of its native instincts; 4) a naturalistic account can be provided of how this enforced introjection might have taken place; and 5) culture (or civilization) is not a permanent fixture of the human condition, but a developmental stage that human beings may yet outgrow. Although he speaks more generally of the 'instincts', moreover, he is particularly concerned in Essay II with the introjection of the instinct for *cruelty*.

Mindful of his emphasis thus far on the bad conscience as an illness, Nietzsche closes this section by celebrating its generative capacity and power. Simply put, the illness of the bad conscience prepared these captive human animals – heretofore formless, soulless and altogether unremarkable – to become rudimentary *persons*, sufficiently advanced toward individuation to be coerced into the primitive contracts described in Sections 4–7. Indeed, here we

encounter an enduring motif of Nietzsche's philosophy: the potentially vivifying power of non-lethal wounds. The sudden appearance
of 'an animal soul turned against itself', he explains, impregnated
the human animal *with a future* that it previously did not possess
and could not have anticipated. Thus began the 'spectacle' of the
human soul, which eventually became sufficiently complex (and
intriguing) that it attracted the attention of 'divine spectators'. As
we shall see, in fact, Nietzsche wishes to distinguish between two
kinds of divine spectator, which correspond to the two kinds of religion (and religious 'spectacle') that he is about to discuss. Here he
alludes to the more promising of these two approaches to religion,
of which he treats the ancient Greeks as exemplary, wherein the self-
inflicted torment endured by noble human beings is explained as satisfying the cruel needs of voyeuristic gods. The other approach,
which he associates with Christian morality, traces this self-inflicted
suffering to an irreparable flaw in human nature itself.

Section 17

Continuing to backtrack, Nietzsche discloses the two 'presupposi-
tions' that support his daring 'hypothesis'. First of all, he explains,
the unprecedented change described in the previous section was
neither 'gradual' nor 'voluntary'. In direct opposition to the gentler
(e.g. adaptation-centred) theories favoured by his rivals, he posits a
sudden, unexpected upsurge of pure activity. He thus explains the
decisive transition described in the previous section in terms of the
capture and containment of a defenceless populace by a pack of
marauding beasts of prey.

As we recall, Nietzsche introduced the designation *beast of prey* to
provide a different perspective on those nobles whom the 'morality of
ressentiment' had pronounced *evil* (GM I: 11). There we encountered
the beasts of prey as they stumbled toward the end of their reign of
terror. Weary from the competing demands of their divided existence,
these weekend warriors were just beginning to take seriously the
charges levelled against them by the increasingly confrontational men
of *ressentiment*. Here, however, we encounter the beasts of prey in
their amoral, form-giving heyday, when they were indistinguishable in
their own eyes, and those of their victims, from rogue forces of nature.
Innocent of 'guilt, responsibility, [and] consideration', these 'born
organizers' worked joyfully and spontaneously to transform the
docile populace they had seized. Their victims suddenly 'enclosed

within the walls of society and peace' (GM II: 16), were thus obliged either to adapt to their new, post-instinctual existence *or* to perish.

Second, the earliest state did not arise as a cooperative venture, as champions of the 'social contract' would have us believe. Rather, the state was founded and maintained 'by nothing but acts of violence'. Politics began, that is, as warcraft by other means, while warcraft developed as a natural outgrowth of the amoral predation practised by the conqueror race. The earliest state thus appeared as a cross between a prison and a menagerie. Its captives were cruelly probed, examined and subjected to the crude, invasive techniques of domestication that are typically associated with the breeding of non-human livestock. Nietzsche thus refers to the earliest state as a 'machine', which ceaselessly, amorally moulded its captive populace into something new, organized and useful. *His* version of the rise of civilization thus emphasizes the experience of loss and trauma that was endured by (most of) those who found themselves immured within peaceful societies. His point in doing so is not to suggest that the advantages of civilization are somehow exaggerated or illusory, but to provide a more balanced reckoning of its advantages and disadvantages for those animals whose survival it secured.

Here we see why it was so important for Nietzsche to insist, first of all, on a distinction between the relatively enduring *procedure* and the relatively fluid *purpose* (or *meaning*) of punishment; and second, on the precedence of the former to the latter (GM II: 13). Having subdued and mastered their captives, these beasts of prey were able to derive a 'fresh interpretation' of the form-giving artistry they had practised all along (GM II: 12). What we now know as *punishment* thus originated, quite unexpectedly, in the gratuitous animal aggression unleashed against a formerly 'shapeless' populace, which somehow managed to survive this attack in a form that was suggestive of its potential utility to its conquerors. The original 'purpose' and 'meaning' of punishment thus arose from a unique enactment (and subsequent interpretation) of its much older, established 'procedure' (GM II: 13). In this particular case, we should note, the precedence of procedure to purpose also marks the passage of the human animal from its pre-civilized, nomadic, instinctual form of existence to its civilized, settled, post-instinctual form of existence.

Nietzsche's story thus directs our attention to the unprecedented pairing of these two peoples. Never before had such a ruthless, aggressive people encountered such a docile, pliable people. Never before had 'artists' of this rank worked in such a responsive medium. Prior to this chance encounter, we are apparently meant to understand, the raids conducted by these predators had produced only corpses, useless victims and wild prisoners unfit for domestication. On this occasion, however, their standard programme of violence unexpectedly yielded victims and captives whom they judged to be potentially receptive to conditions of confinement and domestication.[58] As it turns out, in fact, neither of these complementary peoples was as averse to civilization as his initial description of their 'wilderness' might have led us to conclude (GM II: 16). The beasts of prey were willing and able to keep (rather than kill) their victims, while their victims were willing and able to bear (rather than refuse) the terms of their captivity. Their fateful meeting thus created for the first time the circumstances under which it became both possible and desirable for these 'semi-animals' to be organized – either by themselves or by others – to a degree that exceeded the order afforded them by their instincts and their rudimentary principles of organization.

According to Nietzsche, the founding of the earliest state also created the conditions under which the human animal would eventually contract the illness of the bad conscience. As the beasts of prey conducted their standard programme of violence, they inadvertently left their victims no outlet for the discharge of their own native cruelty. Having survived the sudden transition to peaceful captivity, their victims found that they were now required to turn their animal aggression against themselves. The bad conscience entered the world, Nietzsche thus explains, as an unintended, unanticipated by-product of the 'artistic' cruelty that the beasts of prey amorally visited upon their 'formless' victims. What this section explains, then, is the appearance not of the bad conscience itself, but of its most important precondition – namely, the *conscience*, which, as we have seen, Nietzsche understands as the experience of interiority (or internal duality) that attends the inward discharge of instinctual energy. When obliged by the terms of their captivity to redirect their animal cruelty against themselves, the victims of the predatory aggression described in this section became creatures of conscience.

Although Nietzsche's larger narrative confirms that these victims eventually contracted the compound illness of the bad conscience, there is no reason to believe that they did so immediately upon entering their enforced captivity. In fact, the emergence of the conscience – and, so, the beginning of the human animal's post-instinctual existence – may have preceded the invention of the bad conscience by centuries, perhaps even by millennia. This is possible, as we have seen, because the primitive practice of corporal punishment actually served to postpone the development of the bad conscience (GM II: 14). So long as these creatures of conscience were able to regard their captors as rogue forces of nature – as opposed to evil enemies – they would endure very little of the 'inward pain' that eventually would prompt them to seek the comfort that the bad conscience provides (GM II: 14). They became susceptible to 'inward pain', as we have seen, only when the pursuit of justice called for mercy rather than reprisal (GM II: 10). At that point they were placed in the care of the priest, who encouraged them to interpret their suffering as a just (and therefore meaningful) punishment for their past transgressions.[59]

Section 18

As if to acknowledge the radical nature of his hypothesis, Nietzsche urges his readers not to 'think lightly' of the bad conscience. Proposing a homology between the externally directed 'artistry' of the beasts of prey and the internally directed 'artistry' of their captives, he insists that in both cases,

> it is the same active force that is at work . . . – namely, the *instinct for freedom* (in my language: the will to power).

The discharge of active force is directed in the former case toward external others, and in the latter case toward an internal other – namely, one's 'whole ancient animal sense'. Of course, one's enjoyment of the cruelty visited upon this internal other increases in direct relation to the degree to which one can dissociate oneself from – and, so, demonize – this other.

This is an important elaboration of his initial account of the bad conscience, for it signals his intention to honour the bad conscience as a generative force within the ongoing development of the human animal. Likening this 'illness' to a *pregnancy*, he suggests that it may culminate in the birth of a healthy child (i.e. an extra-moral future for humankind), in a miscarriage (which may or may not bring an end to the civilizing regime of culture), or, more disastrously, in the death of the mother (i.e. the extinction of the human animal in the moral stage of its evolution). As we have seen, each of these outcomes is fully consistent with his general affirmation of the will to power.

Section 19

Once again likening this 'illness' to a pregnancy, Nietzsche invites his readers to join him in 'seeking out the conditions under which this illness has reached its most terrible and most sublime height'. Despite once again neglecting to name Christianity, he thereby announces his intention to explain how the bad conscience came to serve as the basis for the Christian teaching (and experience) of guilt. To this end, he turns now to explain how the creatures of conscience described in Sections 4–10 became the inventors of the *bad* conscience. The key to this explanation is the development of a distinctly *religious* sense of personal responsibility.

Nietzsche resumes his account, suspended in Section 10, of the evolution of the creditor–debtor relationship. As we recall, the self-cancellation of justice allowed him to focus more narrowly on the 'most powerful men' in the community, for whom the 'privilege' of mercy was reserved (GM II: 10). These men, he now explains, served the 'original tribal community' as models for its founding ancestors and subsequently for its gods. He thus sets out to explain how the concepts of *guilt* and *duty* acquired their uniquely *religious* significance. (His account of how they acquired their *moral* significance must wait until Section 21.) In doing so, he continues to chart the growth of the kind of tribe that measures its strength in terms of the magnitude of the debt load that it can bear without penalty or depletion. In the primitive tribal communities under consideration, debt was considered an index of wealth rather than poverty, of strength rather than weakness, of surplus rather than lack.

All such tribes, he offers, 'recognized a juridical duty toward earlier generations, and especially toward the earliest, which founded the tribe'. As the community continued to thrive, it credited the expansion of its power to the founding labours of its ancestors, whom it consequently resolved to repay 'with sacrifices and accomplishments'. As further enhancements of its power led the tribe to fear its ancestors as 'powerful spirits', and eventually as *gods*, the tribe's sense of its indebtedness increased in proportion to the divine patronage it enjoyed. The strongest tribes were eventually compelled to prepare a 'wholesale sacrifice', occasionally involving the 'notorious sacrifice of the first-born'. As we have seen, moreover, it is no accident that these gods were understood to demand the 'festivals' and 'spectacles' of cruelty that thriving tribes were all-too-eager to stage for their enjoyment (GM II: 7).

Nietzsche thus traces the origins of religion to a particular interpretation of the experience of internal duality that accompanies the internal discharge of animal aggression, which, as we have seen, is the non-negotiable opportunity cost incurred by everyone who participates in civil society. Although this particular interpretation is most familiar to us as the basis on which Christianity apportions guilt to alleged sinners, this section discloses the affirmative, pre-moral role of religion in the natural development of a healthy, thriving tribe. A tribe that has managed to pay its debts, vanquish its rivals, ignore its parasites, and honour its founding ancestors requires a novel means of expressing its strength. The self-cancellation of justice thus positions the tribe in question to see itself as indebted to non-human others, and as responsible for honouring extra-contractual obligations.

In describing the emergence of a religious sense of personal responsibility Nietzsche continues to emphasize the enjoyment that strong, healthy human beings naturally derive from the cruelty they visit upon others. The gods were invented, that is, not to curb human suffering, but to encourage healthy, thriving tribes to maintain their good conscience as they mounted ever more ambitious displays of their native cruelty. Revered as 'the friends of *cruel* festivals' (GM II: 7), the earliest gods served to witness – and, so, to justify – the suffering that primitive human beings could not help but inflict upon one another. This may explain why Nietzsche identifies religion as one of the 'inventions' through which life has managed most successfully to justify itself and its resident 'evil' (GM II: 7).

As the strongest tribes became conscious of their debts to supernatural creditors, the concept of debt became increasingly abstract. (Here, no doubt, we may infer the growing influence of the priests, who helped tribal leaders to divine the wishes of the gods.[60]) No longer simply a matter of actual contracts and publicly recorded promises, the debt incurred by the tribe could be reckoned only as a function of its achieved growth and power. As a result, the thriving tribe no longer could anticipate its future obligations; any attempt to budget prudently for future repayments was reduced to guess-work. From this point forward, in fact, there would be no limit either to the magnitude of the debt the tribe could incur or to the sacrifice it would be expected to offer in recompense for its prosperity. This also means, of course, that there was no limit to the enjoyment the tribe could expect to derive from the festivals and spectacles it would stage for its bloodthirsty gods.

This development thus marks an important step in the transformation of the concept of *debt* into the concept of *guilt*. The acquisition of a set of extra-contractual obligations paves the way, first of all, for an expanded role for 'priestly agitators', as in the Second Temple period of the history of Israel (A 25); and, second, for the unlimited, irredeemable debt (= guilt) that Christians assigned to themselves on behalf of their God. Indeed, although Nietzsche continues in this section to chart the growth of a healthy, thriving tribe, his account of the emergence of a distinctly religious set of obligations sets the stage for the invention of the bad conscience. As tribal leaders shifted their attention to the task of satisfying the tribe's religious obligations, they neglected to check the power of the priests, to whom they had mercifully delegated the task of managing the lower orders of society. The priests exploited this opportunity, first of all, by encouraging the unpunished sufferers entrusted to their care to become the inventors of the bad conscience; and second, by encouraging them to interpret their bad conscience as evidence of their guilt. As improbable as it may seem, the self-cancellation of justice thus marks the beginning of the end for the thriving tribe described above.

Nietzsche closes this section by announcing his intention to 'follow to its end the course of this whole development of the consciousness of guilt'. As we shall see in the next section, this announcement also signals his intention to skip over entire millennia, so that he might focus on the dawning of the Common Era. Rather than continue to chart the growth of thriving tribes in the prehistoric period of human development, he instead fast-forwards to the endpoint of this process, where, as we shall see, yet another qualitative change awaits.

Section 20
Nietzsche now situates his account of the origin and development of responsibility against the historical (and pre-historical) background

that he has lightly sketched throughout GM. In an almost comic exercise of historical compression, he asserts that

> the guilty feeling of indebtedness to the divinity continued to grow for several millennia – always in the same measure as the concept of god and the feeling for divinity increased on earth and was carried to its heights.

He thus arrives at 'the advent of the Christian God', which, once named, finally fixes the endpoint of his account of the transformation of the concept of *debt* into the concept of *guilt*.

As presented, this conclusion is more than a bit confusing. Nietzsche appears to place the Christian God at the terminus of the progression he has described thus far in his account of thriving tribes and the evolution of their experience of indebtedness. Based on his analysis thus far, however, the early Christians cannot be said to have *owed* their God anything at all, much less the maximum debt, for they enjoyed none of the material advantages that typically accrued to those tribes whose debt signified the patronage of a strong deity. If we rely on the terms and concepts that Nietzsche has employed thus far in Sections 19–20, the 'maximum feeling of guilty indebtedness on earth' *should* belong to the tribe or people that has amassed and displayed the maximum power to date, as determined by the magnitude of the debt load it can bear without suffering a net depletion of its strength.[61] In terms of the progression he has described thus far, in fact, the advent of the 'maximum god' *should* mean that the healthiest tribe is compelled to sacrifice *itself*, which it might accomplish by extending its dominion beyond its sustainable limits or by waging war simultaneously with several of its chief rivals.

This is precisely why Nietzsche can no longer continue to chart the ascendancy of those thriving tribes whose experience of indebtedness reflects the growth of their power and prosperity. Although these tribes developed a distinctly religious understanding of their debts and obligations (GM II: 19), they did not develop the sense of guilt that Nietzsche has identified as the new focus of his discussion. He will return to this lineage in Section 23, but for now he must turn his attention to a very different lineage, a *decadent* lineage, which is characterized by the desire 'to *reverse* the direction of the development described above' (GM II: 21).

This shift of focus is possible, as we have seen, because the healthy, thriving tribe he has discussed thus far has sown within itself the seeds of its own destruction. As tribal leaders devote themselves to the task of appeasing the tribe's patron deities, they delegate their (formerly pressing) legal obligations to the priests, who are expected to manage the lower orders of society. The acquisition of a distinctly religious set of obligations thus places the tribe in a position of potentially unhealthy dependency on its priestly class. In the worst case, as we shall see, the priests quietly accumulate political capital, which they will spend in the event that tribal leaders fail to sustain the growth of the tribe. It is just such an event that Nietzsche now wishes to examine. Having attained and begun to decline from the apex of its power, the (unnamed) tribe in question wishes above all 'to preclude pessimistically . . . the prospect of a final [i.e. self-sacrificial] discharge' (GM II: 21). The key to his account of this divergent lineage, as we shall see, lies in the decisive reversal that inaugurates the final stage in this process of transformation.

Section 21

Nietzsche begins this section by marking the conclusion of his 'first brief preliminary account', begun in Section 19, of the development and evolution of a distinctly *religious* sense of obligation. Turning his attention to the 'moralization of these concepts', he now wishes to explain how human beings came to acquire a distinctly *moral* sense of obligation, such that they now feel responsible not only for their debts, but also for their indebtedness, i.e. for the inherent limitations and dependencies that are characteristic of their nature. For the purposes of *this* explanation, as we have seen, the healthy, thriving tribe described in Sections 19–20 is of no further use to him.

In a disarming gesture of self-correction, Nietzsche concedes that the hopeful note on which he concluded the preceding section was not entirely warranted. He spoke there, he realizes, 'as if this moralization had not taken place at all', i.e. as if our sense of religious obligation were an uncomplicated bequest from the healthy, noble lineage described in Sections 19–20. Surely, however, it is not. While the widely-hailed 'victory of atheism' may liberate us from our feeling of *indebtedness* to the Christian God (GM II: 20), it does not eradicate our feeling of *guilt* before this God. That we continue to feel guilty before a God in whom we no longer invest our resolute belief is in fact a sign of the predicament that uniquely defines the intended readership of GM. As we shall see, moreover, Nietzsche's (feigned) enthusiasm for the 'victory of atheism' is premature in any event, for he and his unknown friends still have faith in the divine, saving power of truth (GM III: 24). The atheism that would grant us a 'second innocence' has not yet appeared on earth.

Nietzsche's gesture of self-correction also signals his intention to speak more clearly, and more honestly, about Christianity itself, which he has been reluctant thus far to name. His explanation of 'the involvement of the *bad* conscience with the concept of god' is thus meant to recall his claim that Christianity represents the *continuation* – and not, as many believe, the cancellation – of the Jewish revaluation of aristocratic values (GM I: 7). According to Nietzsche, the early Christians both inherited and perfected the Jewish project of perpetrating 'the radical *falsification* of all nature' (AC 25). The slave revolt in morality may have originated in 'Jewish hatred' (GM I: 8), but it came to fruition only with the advent of Christianity, wherein

> God himself sacrifices himself for the guilt of mankind . . . [and] makes payment to himself.

This 'stroke of genius on the part of Christianity', credit for which Nietzsche awards to the apostle Paul,[62] thus marks the completion of the project, begun by the Jewish priests of the Second Temple Period, of invalidating the natural basis for morality and religion. Unlike the thriving, powerful tribe described in Sections 19–20, the early Christians owed their God an altogether different (i.e. denatured) kind of repayment, which, it turns out, he alone could provide on their behalf. There was literally nothing that they could do to repay God for his supposed patronage, which placed him (and them) outside the natural economy of creditor–debtor relations. The Christian God thus qualifies as the 'maximum god attained so far' not only on the basis of what he demanded of his followers, but also on the basis of what he refused to accept from them. Rather than mark an extension of the process of growth through which legal and religious obligations are naturally acquired, that is, the emergence of moral obligations marks a departure from this process.

Nietzsche's argument in this section is extremely compressed. He apparently means to describe two final steps in the transition from *debtor* to *sinner*, and he apparently regards this transition as central

to the fashioning of the particular kind of self that Christian morality both presupposes and produces.[63] First of all, the harrowing
'prospect of a final discharge' compelled these hapless debtors to
'turn back [against themselves] the concepts "guilt" and "duty"',
which in turn required them to contract a relatively stable and
enduring sense of identity, to which *guilt* and *duty* could be meaningfully assigned.[64] Only in that event could these debtors be held
permanently responsible for their deeds, which henceforth would be
known as *sins*.[65] The 'moralization of the concepts guilt and duty'
thus contributed to the consolidation of a new sense of self, which
circumscribed (but did not heal) the experience of self-division,
and which interpreted (but did not alleviate) the pain of the bad
conscience.

Second, these transformed debtors 'turned [these concepts] back
against the "creditor"'. Having learned to hold themselves responsible for failing to pay their debts, the early Christians proceeded to
assign responsibility for their faulted selves to the *'causa prima'*,
which they also construed in terms of humankind itself, a mythical
Alpha progenitor, nature, or existence in general. Pronouncing
themselves '"too good" for this world' (GM III: 1), they placed
themselves (and their goodness) in opposition to the entire known
cosmos. In doing so, they cleverly managed to shift the onus of
repayment to their God. If everything that is not God is tainted, then
God himself must perform the divided office of creditor *and* (proxy)
debtor. The currency in which he repays himself also must be
untainted, which is why he must sacrifice himself, in the person of
his only 'son', to discharge the obligations of his beloved debtors. In
order to receive this macabre token of his love for them, the early
Christians were willing to regard themselves as, and suffer the con-
sequences of being, burdened by the irredeemable debt known as
guilt. With the establishment of Christian morality, that is, sinners
knew themselves to be responsible not only for their promises and
obligations, but also for themselves, i.e. for the very nature of their
faulted existence.

The rise of the Christian God thus completes the transformation
of the concept of *debt* into the concept of *guilt*. To experience oneself
as guilty is to experience oneself as permanently and irremediably
indebted, independent of what God has and has not provided in
recent memory. One stands *guilty* before the God of Christianity,
that is, inasmuch as one's indebtedness to him is indelibly imprinted

onto one's very being. Guilt thus serves as a permanent locus of indebtedness and, so, as an insurmountable barrier to repayment. In other words, *debt* finally became *guilt* when the ancient 'equivalence between injury and pain' (GM II: 4), which had sustained in its entirety the 'prehistoric labor' performed by humankind on itself, was claimed (and believed) no longer to obtain. For this new species of injury, no amount of suffering would provide adequate recompense.

Section 22

Having explained the moralization of the concepts of *guilt* and *duty*, Nietzsche now seeks to divine the underlying truth of this process, as it is reflected in the psychology of the *sinner*. As promised, that is, he is now prepared to disclose 'the conditions under which [the bad conscience] has reached its most terrible and most sublime height' (GM II: 19).

As his readers now understand, there is no need to appeal to the 'paradoxical and horrifying expedient' that underlies Christian theology (GM II: 21). The basic principles of animal–human psychology will suffice. Explicitly linking his explanation to the hypothesis articulated in Sections 16–17, he explains that

> This man of the bad conscience has seized upon the presupposition of religion so as to drive his self-torture to its most gruesome pitch of severity and rigor. Guilt before *God*: this thought becomes an instrument of torture to him.

The caged animal described in Section 16 thus reappears as the self-denying, self-despising Christian sinner. How to account for this transformation? When we last encountered him, this miserable creature had taken the advice of the priest and transformed himself into the inventor of the bad conscience (GM II: 16). Unable to avail himself of 'the *more natural* vent for his cruelty', he interpreted his suffering as the punishment he deserved for harbouring animal instincts. Only thereby was he able to justify (and eventually enjoy) the suffering that he was obliged in any event to inflict upon himself.

Although we have no reason to suppose that the pretext of the bad conscience proved inadequate, we now understand that the caged animal became dissatisfied with it. (As we shall see, he was escorted to this dissatisfaction by the ascetic priest, who intervened for a second time following his realization of the political ends toward which he could mobilize the sufferers entrusted to his care.) According to Nietzsche, the caged animal

> seized on the presupposition of religion so as to drive his self-torture to its most gruesome pitch of severity and rigor. Guilt before *God*: this thought becomes an instrument of torture to him.

Here we may infer the installation of a second, amplified version of the ascetic ideal. No longer content to hold himself responsible for the finite debts he had (supposedly) incurred, the caged animal now wished to hold himself responsible for debts that he would never repay. Having persuaded himself of 'his own absolute unworthiness', he gleefully directed his cruelty against himself, while *also* accepting it, penitently, as his due. His bad conscience was thus transformed into a guilty conscience. Once fully 'moralized', that is, the concept of *debt*, now understood as *guilt*, became an essential, permanent fixture of his divided soul. The sinner's *religious* debts may rise and fall as the power of his God waxes and wanes, but his *moral* obligations (i.e. his guilt) remain constant and irremediable.

The psychological key to the success of this new pretext was the willingness of the caged animal to regard himself as representative of a new species of debtor, for whom the 'ancient equivalence' between debt and punishment did not obtain. In pronouncing himself guilty, that is, the Christian sinner removed himself from the traditional creditor–debtor relationship *and* from the formative 'breeding' process it sponsored. For him, there would be no further articulations of responsibility and no additional opportunities to progress toward self-mastery. While the guilty sinner may appear to assume the maximum burden of responsibility, he in fact makes himself radically irresponsible, for he categorically refuses the burden of any debt that he actually might be expected to repay. Rather than expose himself to a burden of responsibility that *might* prove to be overwhelming, he opts to ensure that his current burden will remain constant and unchanging. He accomplishes this feat, as we have seen, by insisting that his personal sense of responsibility must also be irremediable. He finds himself guilty, that is, as a means of protecting himself from the possibility that he may not prove equal to additional burdens of responsibility. That he also forfeits the opportunity for further growth and development is apparently an acceptable price for him to pay.

Nietzsche thus treats the appearance of the Christian sinner as a deviation from the natural, formative process through which the human animal had thus far contracted its sense of personal responsibility. Weakened by the illness of the bad conscience, and fearful of the prospect of an identity-dissolving 'final discharge', this reluctant debtor resolved to preserve his acquired sense of identity at any expense. So long as he remained a guilty sinner, he was in no danger of acquiring any responsibilities that might crush – or transform – him. In particular, he was unlikely to acquire any obligations to the kind of god whose witness might have stimulated his continued growth and development.

Here we should note that Nietzsche has not yet explained why anyone would voluntarily pronounce himself guilty. Before he can provide this explanation, he first must explain the meaning (and meanings) of the ascetic ideal, which he undertakes in Essay III.

Section 23
Having explained the origin of the 'holy God', which he indirectly promised to do at the end of Section 19, Nietzsche now turns, as he explicitly promised in Section 19, to discuss the 'ennoblement of the gods', which is the process through which thriving tribes and peoples have managed to 'ward off' the bad conscience.

His larger methodological point in this section is to demonstrate that belief in a divinity need not lead, as it does in the case of Christianity, to 'the self-crucifixion and self-violation of humankind'. In particular, he wishes to show that the acquisition of religious obligations need not consign a tribe or people to the arrested development that attends the acquisition of moral obligations. Returning, if only briefly, to his account of the growth and development of healthy tribes, he finally connects the natural progression charted in Sections 19–20 to the emergence of the noble morality in Greek antiquity. According to Nietzsche, the lusty gods of Greek mythology are best understood as

> reflections of noble and autocratic men, in whom *the animal* in man felt deified and did *not* lacerate itself.

Unlike the early Christians, who blamed their animal nature for inclining them toward sin, the noble Greeks honoured their animal nature as indicative of their affinity with (and vulnerability to) their patron gods. The Greeks thus used their gods to inoculate themselves against the 'madness of the will' that afflicted the early Christians. How did they do so?

Like other thriving tribes and peoples, the nobles of Greek antiquity turned inward to discover the cause of their self-inflicted suffering. Having done so, they learned to attribute their suffering to their native *folly*, which, they believed, caused them to suffer an occasional 'disturbance in the head'. But they did not stop there. They eventually determined that their uncharacteristic fits of lunacy were in fact instigated in them by their wicked, jealous gods, whose interest in the human 'spectacle' occasionally became overly enthusiastic and perverse. Having initially turned inward, that is, the ancient Greeks traced their suffering to a cause – folly – that was controlled (and perhaps also implanted) by external forces. Turning outward, they assigned responsibility for their most heinous crimes to their gods, who served, much as the young Nietzsche had schemed to enlist the Christian God (GM P3), 'as the originators of evil'. Doing so enabled them to preclude any temptation to 'moralize' their religious obligations, i.e. to assume the guilt for their finite, dependent nature. Spared the internal inefficiencies that attend the bad conscience, they were free to devote their considerable resources to the ventures – both 'good' and 'wicked' (GM I: 11) – for which their culture became known. They succeeded thereby in contracting a *limited* measure of personal responsibility, such that they could monitor their debts while also allowing for outward expenditures of their will to power.

Whereas the early Christians employed their God to assume responsibility for the debt they owed him, while reserving the guilt for themselves, the noble Greeks enlisted their gods to take on the guilt that otherwise would have accrued to them.[66] While the early Christians engineered for themselves a condition of self-protective stasis, the noble Greeks positioned themselves to continue along their familiar trajectory of self-expressive growth and development. This contrast is thus meant to demonstrate that the 'moralization' of the concept of *debt* is not essential to the nature of religious obligation. As we have seen, in fact, a healthy tribe or people may take on religious obligations precisely in order to relieve the burden of its responsibility.

Section 24

Nietzsche concludes Essay II by entertaining a hypothetical objection, which is posed on behalf of his target audience: 'What are you really doing, erecting an ideal or knocking one down?' He responds with a question of his own, which apparently is meant to encourage his readers to gauge the extent of their progress thus far: 'But have you ever asked yourself sufficiently how much the erection of *every* ideal on earth has cost?' As if to suggest an answer to this question, he then relates a parable, which apparently is meant to confirm that: 1) his 'destruction' of the existing ideal is a necessary precondition of the erection of a new ideal; and 2) the erection of any ideal invariably involves a massive derangement of the accepted canons of truth and reality.

Translating this parable into the familiar terms of his main narrative, he proceeds to clarify the division of labour that the parable is meant to imply. Wondering if 'we modern men' might somehow shift or lighten the historical burden that we currently bear, he diverts our attention to our talent for self-directed cruelty, which he praises as 'our distinctive art' and as a 'subtlety in which we have acquired a refined taste'. It is, in short, what we now do most naturally and effortlessly, and with unrivalled expertise. He thus suggests that we might do something *new*, something different, with our ascetic heritage. This is not simply flattery on his part, for his genealogy of morals confirms that we are heirs to a tradition of inventiveness, subtlety and form-giving power. Might we now harness this power and turn the bad conscience *against* the anti-naturalism it has bred in us?

Here we finally receive the payoff of Essay II: If we were 'strong enough', we could attempt to turn the power of the bad conscience against our acquired complement of '*unnatural* inclinations'. In order to do so, presumably, we would need to cultivate a sense of responsibility that is limited to our anti-natural, anti-affective failings, such as our 'aspirations to the beyond'. In that way, at the very least, we would avoid the trap of assuming responsibility for debts that we know to be irremediable. As it turns out, however, we are not strong enough to attempt the described reversal:

> The attainment of this goal would require a *different* kind of spirit from that likely to appear in this present age: spirits strengthened by war and victory . . . [I]t would require, in brief and alas, precisely this *great health*!

The 'great health' is not discussed at length in GM, but, as this passage suggests, it figures prominently in Nietzsche's larger, post-Zarathustran project.[67] Here he presents the 'great health' as the physiological precondition of any credible attempt to hijack the bad conscience and turn its power against our acquired, anti-affective nature.

While no doubt discouraging to his readers, Nietzsche's reference to the 'great health' helpfully clarifies the likely aims of GM and the readership it is meant to cultivate. The important point here is that 'we moderns' are sufficiently estranged from the 'great health' that we are in no position yet to appreciate, much less embody, its superlative value. Having grown accustomed to the normalcy of sickness (GM III: 14), we must re-acquire an instinctual preference for health and all that it entails. In order to do so, however, we first need to be 'strengthened by war and victory'. Fortunately for us, these catalysts of fortification are right around the corner, for in Essay III of GM Nietzsche wages war on the ascetic ideal. If strengthened sufficiently by our participation in this war, we may join Nietzsche in hosting the final act in the self-overcoming of Christian morality.

We might suppose that Essay II should end here, so that Nietzsche's readers might commence their training in the martial arts and virtues. But it does not end here. Instead, he concludes this section with a surprisingly confident forecast, in which he invokes on several occasions the *necessity* of the future that he envisions:

> But some day, in a stronger age than this decaying, self-doubting present, he must yet come to us, the *redeeming* human being of great love and contempt . . .

If the advent of this redeemer is assured, then Nietzsche and his readers need do nothing to secure the conditions of his arrival. This is good news, inasmuch as we recently have been apprised of our relative lack of strength for such endeavours. We also are assured that the redeemer will come 'to us', which suggests that the prophesied 'stronger age' may not be far off. All we need do, apparently, is to prepare ourselves to receive the redeemer in such a way that positions us to participate in his promised '*redemption* of . . . reality'.[68]

Section 25

Nietzsche cuts short his reverie and retreats into silence. Lest he exceed the limits of what he is entitled to say, he defers to Zarathustra, who is 'younger, "heavier with a future," and stronger' than he.[69] Like his readers, that is, he too must honour the order of rank, which means that he too must accept his assignment to the lesser task that awaits him.

Here we should note, however, that Nietzsche calls himself to order only *after* issuing his reassuring promise of a redemptive future. He apparently does not regard this promise as impermissible, and he expresses no regrets or misgivings for having issued it. To say anything *more* would encroach upon the prerogative of Zarathustra, but what he has said thus far is entirely appropriate. His conscience has asserted itself, that is, but *not* by means of the debilitating, prohibitive, punitive gesture that is most familiar to us.[70] Rather than punish him for wishing to usurp the station of another, his conscience serves notice of his designs on Zarathustra's prerogative. He may not have crossed the line that separates his station from Zarathustra's, but he certainly has marked this line as a site of future contestation. As such, his promise actually confirms his kinship to Zarathustra – who bade his disciples to snatch his wreath (ZI: 22.3) – even as it announces his intention to rival him.

The assertion of Nietzsche's conscience thus suggests that he is *nearly* 'young' enough to say more on this topic, perhaps because, as he says elsewhere, he is 'dangerously healthy, ever again healthy' (GS 382). While he does not possess the great health that will suffuse the redemptive spirits of the future, he is sufficiently advanced in his convalescence to suggest a credible link between 'this decaying, self-doubting present [age]' and the 'stronger age' to come. His audacious promise furthermore suggests the possibility of a conscience whose admonitions we might come to welcome and trust, i.e. of a bad conscience turned good. Intrigued by this gratuitous display of excess strength, in fact, his readers may conclude that Nietzsche is sufficiently healthy not only to continue to guide their voyage of self-discovery, but also to lead them into battle against the ascetic ideal.

Summary

Nietzsche's account of the origin and development of responsibility is meant to disclose the true costs incurred by the human animal in its acquisition of a uniquely moral sense of personal responsibility.

The transformation of the concept of *debt* into the concept of *guilt* reflects a process of development through which the human animal received the unique 'breeding' that has thus far secured its selection for survival. Nietzsche is concerned, however, that the influence of the Christian teaching of guilt has all but negated the salutary, species-preserving effects of this 'breeding'. He fears, in fact, that the unsustainable burden of guilt may very soon consign the human animal to extinction.

Suddenly and forcibly estranged from its natural instincts, the human animal was obliged to endure the inward discharge of its native aggression. Prompted by its self-inflicted suffering to develop a rudimentary sense of self-awareness, the human animal was deemed an apt subject for the investiture of memory. Having thus become a creature of conscience, the human animal subsequently contracted the species-preserving illness of the bad conscience, which rendered meaningful the otherwise meaningless suffering that resulted from the inward discharge of its instincts. Having thus become a creature of the bad conscience, the human animal was further (and dangerously) debilitated by its exposure to Christian morality, through which it contracted the crushing burden of irremediable debt, or *guilt*. Owing to the influence of Christian morality, the human animal now finds itself, *qua* guilty sinner, lacking a will for the future. Although nature has thus far selected the human animal for survival, Nietzsche fears that the cumulative effects of Christian morality will mark the human animal for extinction.

Closing this grim narrative on a more positive note, Nietzsche anticipates a future in which human beings might turn the power of the bad conscience against the anti-affective self-hatred that has been bred in them. This future will be secured by the advent of a mysterious redeemer, who will liberate humankind and reality itself from the curse of the ascetic ideal.

Study questions
1. How does Nietzsche account for the acquisition of memory?
2. How does Nietzsche characterize the institution of punishment prior to the establishment of the state?
3. What is Nietzsche's hypothesis concerning the origin of the 'bad conscience'?
4. How does Nietzsche explain the transformation of the concept of *debt* into the concept of *guilt*?

5. How might Nietzsche's readers turn their 'bad conscience' and ascetic heritage to their own advantage?

ESSAY III: WHAT IS THE MEANING OF ASCETIC IDEALS?

Epigraph

Nietzsche closed Essay II by deferring to Zarathustra, whose speech 'On Reading and Writing' is the source from which the Epigraph to Essay III is extracted (in slightly modified form). After allowing Zarathustra to speak, Nietzsche resumes the main narrative of GM, taking up the question of the *meaning* of ascetic ideals.

This Epigraph thus serves as a bridge between the conclusion of Essay II and the beginning of Essay III. That Zarathustra speaks here of warriors and their virtues should come as no surprise, for Nietzsche revealed at the close of Essay II that the goal of 'wed[ding] the bad conscience to all the *unnatural* inclinations' would be attained only by 'spirits strengthened by war and victory' (GM II: 24). Zarathustra's speech is thus meant to exhort Nietzsche's best readers to become warriors, so that they might strengthen themselves and earn the 'love' of wisdom. Unlike knowledge, which Nietzsche's readers routinely 'bring home' as they please (GM P1), wisdom is reserved for those who prove themselves worthy of its selection. Only by winning the 'love' of wisdom, he thus implies, will his readers contribute to the production of the redemptive future previewed at the close of Essay II. He thus attempts in Essay III to help his best readers to become what wisdom wants in a warrior: *unconcerned*, *mocking* and *violent*.

Section 1

As promised (GM P8), Nietzsche begins Essay III with an 'aphorism', which probably comprises all of Section 1 (minus the concluding call-and-response).[71] This aphorism offers preliminary answers to several versions of the general question posed in the title of Essay III. Of particular interest here is the diversity of meanings conferred by the ascetic ideal, especially with respect to pairings that are germane to the advance of Nietzsche's main narrative. What the ascetic ideal means to the priest, for example, is very different from what it means, on the one hand, to the philosopher, with whom the priest enjoys a close relationship; and, on the other hand, to 'the *majority* of mortals',[72] who turn to the priest for consolation.

Despite the obvious importance of ascetic ideals to the narrative of Essay III, Nietzsche offers his readers no preliminary account of what he understands these ideals to involve. Let us begin, then, with a provisional definition. First of all, a moral *ideal* comprises those virtues, beliefs, habits, practices or activities that are deemed particularly conducive to the pursuit of the highest attainable standard of human flourishing. The installation of a credible ideal thus empowers a morality to enforce the laws, commandments, injunctions, obligations and prohibitions that are determined to be necessary to guide individuals toward a greater good that they may not fully appreciate, much less attain, on their own.[73] It is with reference to an established ideal, in fact, that moralities typically exhort their adherents to improve and perfect themselves.

In all of its various forms, the *ascetic* ideal honours the life of self-surveillance, self-deprivation, and self-castigation as the best, most meaningful (= ideal) life available to human beings. The ascetic ideal thus promises meaning and a sense of purpose to those who most vigorously deny themselves the voluptuary pleasures that human beings typically find most enjoyable. While it is true that the ascetic ideal often grants its adherents worldly rewards, its primary source of attraction is its promise of *extra*-worldly rewards, e.g. eternal salvation, expiation of one's sins, karmic transmigration, revenge against one's former oppressors, and so on. In the case of 'the *majority* of mortals', as we have seen, the ascetic ideal furnishes the means whereby they might 'see themselves as "too good" for this world'.

How do agents of the ascetic ideal persuade prospective adherents to exchange earthly pleasures for the mere promise of heavenly reward? The short answer is that the ascetic ideal degrades earthly pleasures and poisons the enjoyment of them. Prospective adherents are persuaded that they have little to lose and a great deal to gain in the bargain. To assist them in arriving at this conclusion, agents of the ascetic ideal offer to embed them in a 'closed system of will, goal, and interpretation' (GM III: 23), which effectively shuts out the non-ascetic temptations of the larger world. Those who enter this 'closed system' are initiated into a comprehensive, totalizing worldview, in which the stipulated truth of asceticism is presented as intelligible, life-sustaining and impervious to critical scrutiny. Within this closed system, the perfection of ever more exacting disciplines of self-denial will translate into a meaningful existence. The long answer, which Nietzsche provides in Essay III, is that the ascetic ideal promises its adherents the *orgies of feeling* that the ascetic priest has taught them to crave. While the rapture that attends these orgies may be suggestive of an otherworld or afterlife, both the physiology of the sinner and the motives of the priest confirm the secular purview of the ascetic ideal.

According to Nietzsche, the ascetic ideal is now in decline.[74] Dependent for its credibility on the God whose 'death' is becoming increasingly difficult to dispute (GS 343), the ascetic ideal no longer serves as an effective general impetus to self-improvement and self-perfection. While it is true that most of us continue to pursue the ascetic practices to which we have become habituated – e.g. jogging, dieting, scholarship, mechanical labour, fantasy distractions, etc. – very few of us actually believe that these familiar routines of self-deprivation will lead us to salvation. What they *will* lead to, in fact, is what the ascetic ideal has, until recently, hidden from our view. According to Nietzsche, the will to improve oneself through self-deprivation has revealed itself as a will to annihilate oneself, albeit ever so slowly.

Nietzsche's reference in this section to 'the basic fact of the human will, its *horror vacui*' thus sets an ominous tone for Essay III. If human beings would 'rather will *nothingness* than *not* will', then we should not be surprised to learn that a *will to nothingness* lies at the heart of every venture that derives its purpose and meaning from ascetic ideals (GM III: 28).

Section 2

Here Nietzsche takes up the question of *artists*, which is the first 'case' listed in the previous section. He is particularly interested in the case of Richard Wagner (1813–33), who, on the strength of his adherence to ascetic ideals, 'leaped over into his opposite'.[75] His attention to this particular case is by no means arbitrary. Although he does not say so, he once enjoyed a very close relationship with Wagner. Their subsequent estrangement caused him a great deal of pain, even if, as he often insisted, it also facilitated his development as an individual thinker in his own right.

Nietzsche begins his analysis by challenging the very basis of Wagner's leap into his opposite: '[T]here is no necessary antithesis between chastity and sensuality.' Where there *is* an antithesis, moreover, it need not be tragic in nature, for 'it is precisely such "contradictions" that seduce one to existence'. Nevertheless, Wagner finally came to 'worship chastity' and resolved to 'set to music' the antithesis that defined him. Nietzsche thus reduces Wagner's asceticism to two basic principles: 1) one must choose between chastity and sensuality; and 2) one should choose chastity.

Section 3
Turning now to investigate the 'opposite' into which Wagner supposedly leaped, Nietzsche focuses on Wagner's *Parsifal*, which was first performed in Bayreuth in 1882.[76] What was *Parsifal* to Wagner? Before providing his answer, Nietzsche whimsically conjectures that

> One might be tempted to suppose . . . that the Wagnerian *Parsifal* was intended cheerfully, as a kind of epilogue and satyr play.

A *Parsifal* born of good cheer would be a sign of Wagner's excess strength and renascent health, much as GM itself is supposed to bear witness to Nietzsche's own convalescence (GM P7). If one cannot imagine *Parsifal* as a crowning exercise in self-mockery, he thus implies, one is obliged to detect in Wagner's 'leap' an attempt at 'self-negation' and 'self-cancellation'.

Section 4
Generalizing from this analysis of Wagner, Nietzsche cautions his readers always 'to separate an artist from his work'. If Wagner is merely the 'precondition of his work', he should not be considered an authority on it. If we wish to understand *Parsifal* or any other artistic production, we should turn instead to the 'physiologists and vivisectionists of the spirit',[77] whose select company, we soon will learn, includes Nietzsche. From this point forward, in fact, he consistently interprets works of art as symptoms of the underlying physiological condition of the artists who produce them. In likening Wagner to a 'pregnant woman', moreover, he sets up an instructive contrast between the miscarriage of *Parsifal* and the healthy pregnancies under way in the 'maternal' philosophers whom he discusses in Sections 8–10.

Section 5
Nietzsche begins this section by repeating once again the first sentence from Section 1, which signals his wish to begin his investigation anew. He then moves to 'eliminate the artists' from

consideration, as they are always dependent on other authorities. Having narrowed the focus of his investigation, he now takes up a 'more serious question: what does it mean when a genuine *philosopher* pays homage to the ascetic ideal?' With the introduction of the philosopher, that is, Nietzsche shifts the focus of his investigation from *ascetic ideals* to the *ascetic ideal*.

Before turning to this question, however, he offers an instructive explanation of Wagner's embrace of Schopenhauer. According to Nietzsche, Schopenhauer persuaded Wagner that music need not find its value in the service of the greater goal of drama, but could be considered an 'independent art' in its own right. Schopenhauer's doctrine of the '*sovereignty* of music' thus encouraged Wagner to inflate the 'value of the *musician* himself', who, Wagner was understandably pleased to learn, could be enlisted to serve as 'God's ventriloquist'. Thus did Schopenhauer assist 'the aged Wagner' in yielding to the '*typical velleity* of the artist' (GM III: 4). As we shall see, Nietzsche will return to this interpretation of the fantasy (or illusion) of independence – namely, as an expression of impotence and self-contempt – in his profile of the ascetic priest.

Section 6

Having exposed Wagner's dependence on Schopenhauer, Nietzsche now reveals the extent of Schopenhauer's dependence on the German philosopher Immanuel Kant (1724–1804). Schopenhauer inherited Kant's formulation of the 'aesthetic problem', which means that, like Kant, he mistakenly assumed the priority of the perspective of the spectator to that of the artist. (A central claim of Nietzsche's theory of art is that the 'monological' perspective of the artist is superior to the 'dialogical' perspective of the spectator (GS 367).)

Nietzsche frames the issue by contrasting Kant's definition of beauty (i.e. as that 'which gives us pleasure *without interest*') with that of Stendhal (1783–1842) (i.e. as that which 'promises happiness' and, so, '*arouses the will*'). Schopenhauer understood Kant to mean 'without *sexual* interest', and, hating the distractions introduced by sexual desire, sided with Kant. Nietzsche speculates that Schopenhauer's entire interest in 'redemption from the will', which is a prominent theme in his classic work, *The World as Will and Representation* (1819), may reflect his very personal wish to be liberated from the unwanted intrusions of sexual desire.

As it turns out, then, Schopenhauer was confused about his allegiance to Kant. In fact, Schopenhauer was an *extremely* interested party. Just as Nietzsche earlier generalized from the case of Wagner, so he now generalizes from the case of Schopenhauer. Here he submits a preliminary answer to 'the more serious question' that he posed in Section 5: the philosopher pays homage to ascetic ideals because 'he wants *to gain release from a torture*'. As we shall see in the next section, this generalization provides the basis for his discussion of the meaning of ascetic ideals for philosophers. According to Nietzsche, philosophers typically misunderstand the nature of their own relationship to the ascetic ideal. This misunderstanding (or self-deception) has served them well thus far, but very soon it will exhaust its usefulness to their development.

Section 7

Nietzsche urges his readers not to become 'gloomy' at the sound of the word *torture*. Echoing his earlier wish for Wagner's *Parsifal* (GM III: 3), he insists that here, too, there is 'even something to laugh at'. As it turns out, in fact, the torture from which Schopenhauer sought release was by no means inimical to his flourishing. Schopenhauer '*needed* enemies in order to keep in good spirits', which is why he treated sexual desire 'as a personal enemy'. His 'anger' at his enemies was in fact his 'reward', his 'happiness'. (This means that Schopenhauer both wished and expected to be paid for his virtue.) His supposed torture thus produced in him the effect that Nietzsche earlier attributed to the contradictions that human beings typically embody (GM III: 2), for it 'seduced him ever again to existence'. In refusing to leap over into his opposite, Schopenhauer cultivated a practice of asceticism that Nietzsche clearly prefers to the self-destructive asceticism of Wagner. Had Wagner paid closer attention, in fact, he might have noticed that (and how) Schopenhauer exploited to his own advantage the tension between chastity and sensuality.

Nietzsche now moves to discuss what is not unique to Schopenhauer, but 'typical' of all philosophers. While Schopenhauer may have been confused about his allegiance to Kant, the two philosophers nevertheless shared a 'peculiar . . . irritation at and rancor against sensuality', which reflects more generally 'a peculiar philosophers' prejudice and affection in favor of the whole ascetic ideal'. Philosophers are drawn to the ascetic ideal, he explains, because it

NIETZSCHE'S *ON THE GENEALOGY OF MORALS*

provides them with the 'optimal conditions' under which they might pursue their reflective deliberations.

In order to support this more general point, Nietzsche helps himself to the depth-psychological model that he introduced in Essay II, to which he now adds welcome detail:

> every animal . . . instinctively strives for an optimum of favorable conditions under which it can expend all its strength and achieve its maximum feeling of power . . .

Drawing on this general principle of animal psychology, he explains the fondness of philosophers for the ascetic ideal in terms of the *instrumental* value they derive from it. Just as Schopenhauer denied the value of existence as a means of affirming his own release from the supposed torture of sexual desire, so philosophers in general embrace the ascetic ideal – represented here by an aversion to marriage and marital sexuality – as a means of affirming themselves and their solitary, spiritual endeavours.

As this reference to the basic principles of animal psychology is meant to emphasize, moreover, the philosopher *instinctively* – as opposed to *consciously* or *deliberately* – embraces the ascetic ideal as a condition of his most meaningful expenditure of strength. This means, as we shall see, that the philosopher typically misunderstands the nature of his relationship to the ascetic ideal. As it turns out, many philosophers take themselves to be devotees of the ascetic ideal when in fact they simply use the ascetic ideal to further their inner growth and development. In the case of philosophers, that is, the ascetic ideal can be an effective means of pursuing (and attaining) the worthwhile, extra-ascetic end of enhanced spirituality.

Section 8

As the case of Schopenhauer reveals, philosophers are *not* disinterested after all, for 'they think of *themselves*'. Their practice of asceticism in fact exemplifies the selfishness (or egoism) that Nietzsche wishes to promote as a healthier alternative to the selflessness (or altruism) that is prized by contemporary morality (GM P5).

These philosophers are of interest to Nietzsche because they deny and deprive themselves in the service of their aspirations to self-improvement and self-perfection. Here it becomes clear, in fact, that he wishes to isolate a productive practice of asceticism, wherein 'great, fruitful, inventive spirits' may find 'the most appropriate and natural conditions of their *best* existence'.[78] To this end, he avails himself once again of the image of *maternity*, which, as we shall see, facilitates the contrast he wishes to draw between these fruitful philosophers and their unsuspecting sponsor, the barren ascetic priest. He insists here that a philosopher deprives himself for the same reasons that an expectant mother deprives herself – namely, to deliver concentrated nurture to that which grows within:

> His 'maternal' instinct, the secret love of that which is growing in him, directs him toward situations in which he is relieved of the necessity of thinking *of himself*.[79]

The 'maternal' philosopher thus cultivates a practice of extreme selfishness, but without attending consciously or reflectively to himself. Selfishness, that is, has very little to do with self-awareness, which is why Nietzsche does not chide his target audience for failing to 'seek' and 'find' themselves (GM P1).[80]

The 'secret love' of the 'maternal' philosophers is thus responsible for guiding their practice of asceticism into apparent – *but in fact productive* – conformity with the ascetic ideal.[81] Although they honour the virtues of 'poverty, humility, [and] chastity', they do so only at the behest of their 'dominating instinct' – namely, their spirituality – and only to divert attention from its pursuit of a greater end, which, for now, must remain hidden from their view. Philosophers qualify as 'maternal', that is, to the extent that they yield – albeit unconsciously and unwittingly – to the 'supreme lord' who resides *within* them. This achievement places them squarely within the lineage of the sovereign individual, who, as we have seen, called his own 'dominating instinct' by the name of *conscience* (GM II: 2). In the case of 'maternal' philosophers, that is, the ascetic ideal means that creatures of conscience need not be burdened by an oppressive bad conscience.

In yet another reference to this lineage, Nietzsche observes that the ascetic ideal sponsors in these 'maternal' philosophers the 'cheerful asceticism of an animal become fledged and divine, floating above life rather than in repose'. This reference is indeed auspicious, for it links these philosophers to the nobles of Greek antiquity, who, we recall, managed to balance their religious obligations in such a way that '*the animal* in man felt deified' (GM II: 23). This echo of

Essay II thus confirms that the 'maternal' philosophers have similarly managed to cultivate ascetic practices that restrain, but do not target for elimination, their animal instincts. Like the noble Greeks, that is, they engage only in those ascetic practices that allow them to pursue productive, extra-ascetic ends. As we shall see, in fact, Nietzsche presents the gestation of *spirit* within the 'maternal' philosophers as culminating, perhaps, in the birth of the new philosopher, who, after the fashion of the emergent butterfly, soon will take wing (GM I: 10).

Taken together, these positive images of the human animal depict the Western moral tradition as sheltering a secret lineage of productive asceticism, through which nature may yet complete its oft-detoured project of breeding an animal that is permitted to make meaningful promises. Indeed, we are now in a position to understand why Nietzsche earlier claimed 'that today there is perhaps no more decisive mark of a *"higher nature"*, a more spiritual nature', than that of hosting a productive clash between the opposing value-systems associated, respectively, with Rome and Judea (GM I: 16). In this light, in fact, the Western moral tradition appears as a grand, desperate experiment in the digestion and incorporation of the potentially lethal poison known as *spirit*.

Section 9

Nietzsche now takes up the question of the origin and development of philosophy itself, with the aim of establishing the *contingent* nature of its dependency on the ascetic ideal.[82] Having noted already the 'fondness' with which 'philosophers have always discussed the ascetic ideal', he now reveals that the 'bond between philosophy and the ascetic ideal is even much closer and stronger' than we might have surmised. He nevertheless wishes to maintain that philosophers have *used* the ascetic ideal, albeit unwittingly, to guard their most important secret.

Exchanging metaphors of reproduction for those of child-rearing, Nietzsche now imagines the ascetic ideal as the parent or guardian of the toddler philosophy. Philosophy began as a 'bad thing', and aspiring philosophers prudently cultivated with respect to themselves the distance and disinterest that would allow them to continue this forbidden practice without identifying themselves with it. They were aided in this process of self-estrangement by the ascetic ideal, which taught them to dissociate themselves from their evil

wishes and impulses. This long process of self-estrangement has cul-
minated in the faulted identity of those 'knowers' whom Nietzsche
addresses in his Preface to GM (GM P1).

Nietzsche's final inference is not stated explicitly, but it is clear
enough: now that philosophy is no longer regarded as such a 'bad
thing', the patronage of the ascetic ideal is no longer needed, especially at such a prohibitive cost. Philosophers now may dare to
reclaim their 'feelings' and 'experiences' and thereby become something other than 'strangers' to themselves (GM P1). In doing so,
moreover, they finally may become fully individuated in their own
right, thereby ending their protracted dependence on the ascetic
priest.

Section 10

How did these 'maternal' philosophers acquire their predilection for
unwitting self-nurture? Drawing on his account of the emergence of
'the contemplative man', Nietzsche explains that philosophers have
followed in the footsteps of their predecessor and sponsor, the priest.

The 'earliest philosophers', he explains, sought above all to
provoke *fear* in others. Mistrusted for their deviation from established customs and traditions, the earliest contemplatives were
obliged to protect themselves from the threat of exile while also
securing the conditions under which they might conduct their
inward reveries without distraction (D 42). They managed to do so
by turning a universally approved practice – the infliction of cruelty
– against themselves. Through the use of 'cruelty toward themselves
[and] inventive self-castigation', the earliest philosophers (e.g.
Brahmins) persuaded others to fear them and leave them alone.[83]
Like the priests, moreover, the earliest philosophers also sought
relief from self-doubt and self-recrimination, especially inasmuch as
they knew themselves to stand in defiance of all known values and
laws. Indeed, the internal distance created by their self-inflicted
cruelty was just as important to their development as the external
distance it afforded them. So it was, Nietzsche suggests, that the earliest philosophers learned to employ 'previously established' ascetic
practices – especially those perfected by the priest – in the service of
their extra-ascetic ends.

In order to take full advantage of this opportunity, of course, the
philosopher was obliged 'to *represent*' the ascetic ideal, which means
that he also 'had to *believe* in it'. Here Nietzsche needs to be very

careful, for he wishes to maintain that the philosopher's 'pose' was both credible – even to the philosopher himself – and yet in some sense contrived.[84] The important point here is that the relationship of philosophy to the ascetic ideal has always allowed for a certain degree of independence, which, until now, has gone undetected. We now learn that some philosophers have unwittingly managed to exploit their independence from the ascetic priest and the ascetic ideal to shelter their secret cultivation of spirit. They have been sufficiently successful in this venture, moreover, that they are now poised to outgrow – and subsequently to renounce – the patronage of the ascetic priest. By the time the ascetic priest finally enters the narrative of GM, in fact, he is ripe for overthrow by the very philosopher whom he has groomed to carry on his work. All this philosopher needs, apparently, is to be made aware of the conditional nature of his allegiance to the ascetic ideal and of his independence from the ascetic priest. This may be why Nietzsche reveals the preferred ending of his story, thereby notifying victor and vanquished alike of his expectations for them.

Nietzsche's depiction of the new philosopher as a skittering butterfly recalls his earlier reference to the 'floating' philosopher, in whom the 'animal' becomes 'fully fledged' and feels itself to be 'divine' (GM III: 8). In both cases, Nietzsche makes productive use of images of natural maturation. The appearance of the new philosopher, we apparently are meant to believe, will occur as naturally as the fledging of a raptor or the emergence of a butterfly from its chrysalis. In both cases, moreover, the maturation in question will assume a monstrous, grotesque aspect. For the uninitiated, there can be no expectation that a scrawny, featherless chick will develop into a magnificent raptor, or that the ugly caterpillar and uglier cocoon will yield a colourful butterfly. The same is true, Nietzsche thus implies, of the ongoing development of the human animal, whose burdensome bad conscience may yet evolve into the seat of sovereignty.[85]

The advent of this new philosopher thus stands as a symbol, and perhaps also as a promise, of our liberation from the 'closed system' of the ascetic ideal. As the image of metamorphosis suggests, the appearance of the new philosopher would reveal that the ascetic priest is in fact a 'caterpillar', i.e. a self-cancelling stage in the natural gestation of spirit, and that the ascetic ideal is a 'cocoon', i.e. an incubator of new forms of life. In that event, the appearance of the new philosopher would demonstrate that the ascetic priest is *not* barren after all, and that the ascetic ideal may yet beget an *open* system. Nietzsche's sketch of the new philosopher thus calls to mind two earlier promises of liberation: 1) his appeal to the survivors of morality, who will announce, cheerfully, that 'our old morality too is part *of the comedy!*' (GM P7); and 2) his invocation of the 'victor over God and nothingness' who will redeem us from the ascetic ideal (GM II: 24).

This is not to suggest, however, that Nietzsche issues an unambiguous promise of liberation. The rhetorical questions that conclude this section may buoy our hopes for the appearance of the new philosopher, but they also raise the serious concern that, as yet, the conditions of this metamorphosis may not obtain. Once again, that is, Nietzsche's conscience has asserted itself, cautioning him not to issue impermissible promises about the future. Rather than grow discouraged, however, Nietzsche is emboldened by his conscience to *do* something. If he cannot become the new philosopher, he must facilitate the emergence of this philosopher in others.

In pursuing this end, he has three options. He may strive to quicken the spirituality that the 'maternal' philosophers secretly nurture within themselves; or he may cultivate the external conditions – the 'sunnier, warmer, brighter world' – that are most hospitable to the release of this 'dangerous winged creature'; or, more drastically, he may hasten the demise of the ascetic ideal and thereby compel the appearance of the new philosopher. While it is likely that Nietzsche means to pursue all three of these strategies, the third option is most germane to the advancing narrative of GM. Once the new philosopher is finally deprived of his sheltering 'cocoon', he will have no choice but to establish a fully individuated existence. As we shall see, in fact, Nietzsche's assault on the ascetic ideal is meant to excise a particularly persistent piece of degenerating life, so that the whole of life may once again flourish as a result.

Here, as elsewhere in the text of GM, form and content coincide. If Nietzsche is to contribute to the emergence of the new philosopher, he must separate himself from the ascetic priest and thereby establish an individuated existence of his own. As we shall see, his case against the ascetic ideal requires him to demonstrate, first, that he and the ascetic priest are intimately related, especially inasmuch as they both serve the 'deepest interests' of life itself; and second, that their common service to life has steered them into diametric opposition to one another. His own efforts to separate himself from the ascetic priest are thus meant both to anticipate and to facilitate the emergence of the new philosopher.

Section 11

At this point in his narrative, Nietzsche shifts his focus from a survey of what the ascetic ideal means in individual cases to the meaning of the ascetic ideal itself. He thus confirms that Sections 1–10 were meant to prepare his readers to meet 'the actual *representative of seriousness*', whose '*right* to exist stands or falls with [the ascetic] ideal'. Unlike the philosopher, who adopts a serious 'pose' while secretly cultivating spirituality, the ascetic priest is serious by nature and necessity. He could not possibly cultivate a cheerful, 'maternal' asceticism, and he never could treat the ascetic ideal as merely a disposable 'mask' or 'cloak' (GM III: 10).

Although Nietzsche treats the ascetic priest as a uniquely defined species of the contemplative type, the narrative of GM attests to four stages in the historical development of this species. As we shall see, in fact, this development is integral to the particular narrative that Nietzsche wishes to relate in GM.

- Appointed by life to tend to the sickliest of human beings, the ascetic priest urged his followers to search within themselves for the cause of their existential suffering. They suffered, he proposed, because they deserved to suffer, as a punishment for their unpaid debts and broken promises. As a result of this first intervention on the part of the ascetic priest, the *bad conscience* became the dominant interpretation of the self-inflicted suffering (or conscience) that attends the inward discharge of animal aggression. In this initial stage of development, the ascetic priest was content to protect the sickly sufferers entrusted to his care. By organizing them into a misery-loving herd, he succeeded in separating them, as was his charge, from the healthy.
- Rather than accept the inevitable decline of Israel from the apex of its power and prosperity, the Jewish priests of the Second Temple Period denatured the concepts of God and morality (A 25–6), thereby launching the slave revolt in morality. While continuing to provide for the sufferers entrusted to their care, the Jewish priests also began to explore the political uses to which they might put the herd, through which they eventually would pursue their personal agenda of revenge.

- Interpreting the crucifixion of Christ as an expression of God's love, the apostle Paul convinced his followers to find themselves (and others) *guilty*, i.e. responsible for the flawed nature of their very being. This teaching marks the second intervention of the ascetic priest, by means of which *guilt* became the dominant interpretation of the illness of the bad conscience. As we shall see, the advantage of pronouncing oneself guilty lies in the access one gains thereby to the *orgies of feeling* that the priest has taught his sinners to crave.
- With the death of God, the authority of the ascetic priest has declined considerably. The 'affect medication' he dispenses is no longer widely sought as a means of attaining salvation, though it is sought and consumed for other reasons. The ascetic priest remains influential only within the limited context of a dwindling audience of truth-seeking scholars. This stage of development finds the ascetic priest at the nadir of his power, which Nietzsche eagerly interprets as a sign that the new philosopher soon may assert his independence from the ascetic ideal. In that event, the ascetic priest would be revealed as having contributed to the survival of the human animal as it enters the extra-moral stage of its development.

While introducing the ascetic priest, Nietzsche floats the 'supposition' that *he and his readers* are (or will become) 'antagonists' and 'deniers' of the ascetic ideal.[86] In order to engage the ascetic ideal in what he elsewhere identifies as the 'final battle' of its long career (GS 358), Nietzsche and his readers must prepare themselves to endure the fury of the ascetic priest, while also resisting the temptation to reciprocate his 'antagonism' towards them. Their goal vis-à-vis the ascetic priest is not to vanquish him, but to *use* him – e.g. as a 'magnifying glass' (EH: 'wise' 7) – to get clearer about the meaning of the ascetic ideal. To this end, in fact, '[they] will need to help him defend himself against [them]', which means that they will need to understand him better than he understands himself. Nietzsche's defence of the ascetic priest (as an agent in the service of life) begins here and continues through Section 16. His subsequent critique of the ascetic priest (as an ersatz physician) comprises Sections 17–21.

Their opposition to the ascetic ideal is directed, he continues, at the '*valuation* placed by the ascetic priest on our life'. Here Nietzsche trains his focus on the metaphysical dualism that has become emblematic of ascetic philosophy and religion. According to the priest, there is another, 'quite different mode of existence', from which one is excluded – *unless* one turns against life and denies its value. Anyone who embraces this teaching is entitled to regard life 'as a bridge to that other mode of existence'. Dedicating oneself to a life of self-denial thus became the price of admission to a wondrous afterworld.

In response to his own question about the 'meaning' of the ascetic mode of valuation, Nietzsche treats his readers to a provisional formulation of his main thesis in Essay III. The persistence of the ascetic priest means that 'it must be in the *interest of* life itself that such a contradictory type does not die out'. Rather than specify the nature of this interest, however, Nietzsche moves instead to establish the various ways in which the ascetic life in fact involves a self-contradiction. His basic point here is that an ascetic life derives its meaning and vitality from its attack on the value of life itself, such that it

> grows more self-confident and triumphant the more its own presupposition, its physiological capacity for life, *decreases*.

Inasmuch as an ascetic life is affectively invested in the destruction of its own precondition, moreover, it harbours what Nietzsche elsewhere calls a *will to nothingness*. This means, as we shall see, that the ascetic ideal in fact sponsors a long, gradual process of self-annihilation. Its promise of afterworldly reward is but a pretext, designed to shield its practitioners from the underlying truth of their adopted regimen of self-deprivation.

Section 12

Nietzsche now turns to consider how this 'incarnate will to contradiction' might be inclined to philosophize. We should not be surprised to learn that this kind of philosophizing invariably esteems appearance over reality, inwardness over physicality, ideality over actuality, and abstraction over concretion. It attains its apotheosis in the 'ascetic self-contempt and self-mockery of reason' that Nietzsche associates with Kant's famous thesis in his *Critique of Pure Reason* (1781 'A'/1787 'B').

Rather than simply dismiss this contrary species of philosophizing, however, Nietzsche informs his readers, whom he identifies once again as fellow 'knowers',[87] that they should be grateful for such obvious contradictions. This ability to reverse perspectives is in fact part of the training they are meant to receive in GM, especially in so far as it contributes to

> the discipline and preparation of the intellect for its future 'objectivity' – the latter understood not as 'contemplation without interest' (which is a nonsensical absurdity),[88] but as the ability to have *control* over one's Pro and Con and to dispose of them, so that one knows how to employ a variety of perspectives and affective interpretations in the service of knowledge.

Even by Nietzsche's standards, this is an extremely dense passage.[89] Let us restrict ourselves here to five observations. First of all, the 'resolute reversals of accustomed perspectives' that he attributes here to Kant – and later, to Schopenhauer[90] – are presented as exemplary in form of the kind of reversals that he expects his readers to be able, eventually, to execute. Second, the recommended 'discipline and preparation of the intellect' must evince an irreducibly *affective* predilection. It is not enough simply 'to see differently in this way', as if, for example, as a matter of hypothetical speculation; one must also '*want* to see differently'. Third, 'objectivity' is an appropriate goal for seekers of knowledge, but not if understood, *à la* Kant, 'as "contemplation without interest"'. Rather than attempt to eliminate all traces of interest and partiality, we should indulge our interests and partialities, allowing them to inform and direct our pursuit of knowledge. Fourth, a greater degree of familiarity with one's interests will acquaint one with 'one's Pro and Con' with respect to any particular topic or question. This is a crucial component of the training under way in GM, for the 'objectivity' of one's knowledge is presented here as a function of one's 'ability to *control* one's Pro and Con and to dispose of them'. Fifth, 'objectivity' is attainable only by those philosophers who 'see' things from multiple perspectives, for its attainment presupposes that one 'knows how to employ a variety of perspectives and affective interpretations in the service of knowledge'.

Continuing to express a deepening sense of intimacy with his readers, Nietzsche now addresses them, formally and deferentially, as 'my dear philosophers'. This particular mode of address in fact marks the achievement of an important milestone in the training of his readers. He recently concluded an extended discussion of philosophers, wherein he identified a 'maternal' lineage that relies on ascetic practices to secure the optimum conditions of enhanced spirituality. More importantly, he has conjectured that this lineage may soon branch off from the priestly lineage that has sponsored its nurture thus far. In addressing his readers as *philosophers*, that is, he may be urging them to join him in declaring their independence from the ascetic priest.

At the same time, however, he also knows that his readers are indebted to the contrary species of philosophizing that he has associated with Kant and Schopenhauer. In preparation for the ensuing investigation of the ascetic ideal, he thus cautions them (and himself) to 'be on guard against the dangerous old conceptual fiction' that beguiled these two venerable philosophers.[91] This fiction promotes the belief that there is only one kind of 'seeing', only one kind of 'eye', and that 'seeing' properly requires us to neutralize (or, more drastically, to divest ourselves of) those 'active and interpreting forces, through which alone seeing becomes seeing *something*'.

In an effort to combat this fiction, he famously counters that 'there is *only* a perspective seeing, *only* a perspective "knowing"'. His general lesson for these 'knowers' is that the pursuit of knowledge necessarily trades upon affect, interest and will. Any movement in the opposite direction – toward disaffection, disinterest and impartiality – will not only arrest the pursuit of knowledge, but also threaten to 'castrate the intellect'.[92] He thus recommends to his readers a pursuit of knowledge that would require their serial access to multiple modes of embodiment, each of which yields a unique perspective.[93] His writ of caution against this 'dangerous old conceptual fiction' thus doubles as an invitation to his readers to open themselves to the larger world around them, to permit their affects to introduce a greater – and, so, more 'objective' – measure of the complexity of experience. He thus urges his fellow philosophers to experience – that is, to embody – their 'Pro and Con', and then to 'control' and 'dispose' of them. Very soon, as we shall see, he will provide them with an example of just how to do so.

Section 13

Treating the previous section as a digression from his main narrative, Nietzsche returns to his consideration of 'our problem', which, as he confirmed in Section 11, pertains to the meaning of ascetic ideals. Having earlier referred to the 'self-contradiction' embodied by an 'ascetic life' (GM III: 11), he now corrects himself, claiming that this self-contradiction is only *apparent*. The ascetic life has been classified as a self-contradiction, he explains, because its 'real nature' has heretofore defied explanation and description. Intending to fill a conspicuous 'old *gap* in human knowledge', he now adopts the perspective of the *physiologist*, from which he conducts his war against the ascetic ideal and his investigation of the ascetic priest.

The significance of this shift in perspective can hardly be exaggerated, for it is only as a physiologist that Nietzsche can assess the full extent of the damage wrought by the ascetic priest and the ascetic ideal. Nor should we take lightly his decision to adopt the most rigorously scientific perspective available to him, for, as he explains elsewhere, 'the priest knows only one great danger: that is science, the sound conception of cause and effect' (A 49). Speaking now from the sophisticated vantage point of the physiologist, he delivers one of the most novel insights recorded in Essay III:

> *[T]he ascetic ideal springs from the protective and healing instincts*[94] *of a degenerating life* which tries by all means to sustain itself and to fight for its existence . . . [T]he ascetic ideal is an artifice for the *preservation* of life.

Here we may appreciate the use to which he employs the alternative theory of life that he introduced in Essay II. As a natural assertion of its dominion, life itself sponsors the ascetic ideal and authorizes its deprecation of the value of life. Through the artifice of the ascetic ideal, that is, life enables the sickliest of human beings to derive a sense of meaning and vitality from their otherwise meaningless suffering. As this passage confirms, in fact, the hallmark of Nietzsche's physiological perspective is the prerogative it grants him to advocate on behalf of the deeper 'interests' of life itself.

Turning explicitly to a physiological consideration of the ascetic ideal, he now reveals the 'great fact' that is expressed by its enormous influence over the course of European civilization. The historical 'power' of this ideal in fact attests to 'the *sickliness* of the type of human being we have had hitherto, or at least of the tamed human being'. That so many human beings partake so eagerly of the ascetic ideal thus means, first of all, that sickness has become epidemic, even *normal*; second, that life itself has dispatched this ideal in an effort to preserve these sickly beings; and third, that the ascetic ideal has been prescribed to a much larger clientele than it could possibly serve.

Nietzsche now turns abruptly to a consideration of the ascetic priest, whom he characterizes as 'the incarnate desire to be different, to be in a different place'. This desire is frustrated, he explains, by the service into which it has been pressed by life itself, which uses the ascetic priest to convince the sickliest of human beings not to give up on life. The priest accomplishes this task by furnishing his sickly sheep with a collective identity (namely, as a herd) and a collective will (namely, to gain revenge in the afterlife). *His* desire to be elsewhere, duly frustrated and sublimated, thus galvanizes *their* will to live, if only so that they might earn the reward that awaits them 'in a different place'. On the strength of this physiological analysis, Nietzsche declares that the 'ascetic priest . . . is among the greatest *conserving* and yes-creating forces of life'.

Without elaborating on this startling declaration, he returns to his discussion of the 'sickliness' that afflicts humankind. In response to his own question concerning its origins, he points to the 'courageous' predilection of human beings for grisly self-experimentation. But this explanation does not really answer the question of *why* human beings are so sick. To complete his argument, he thus reveals *how* the ascetic ideal actually promotes the affirmation of life:

> The No [the ascetic human being] says to life brings to light, as if by magic, an abundance of tender Yeses; even when he *wounds* himself . . . the very wound itself afterward compels him *to live*.

Nietzsche's reference here to *magic* is noteworthy, for he later refers to the ascetic priest as a *sorcerer* (GM III: 15, 20). His allusion to a vivifying wound is also significant, for he later explains that the ascetic priest is obliged to infect the wounds that he both inflicts and salves (GM III: 15).

Nietzsche's transition to the ascetic priest earlier in this section may have been abrupt, but its logic is now clear enough: the ascetic priest is responsible for compounding the sickliness of those human beings whom life has appointed him to serve, and for spreading this sickliness to other, healthier human beings. As we shall see, in fact, the ascetic priest has figured out how to serve the 'deepest interests' of life while also serving his own interests.

Section 14

Here Nietzsche refers to what his readers supposedly know and 'cannot deny', which suggests that he now regards them as possessing a discriminating sense of the order of rank among human types. Unlike the mob-friendly 'democrat' who earlier claimed to 'love the poison' (GM I: 9), his readers are now in a position to appreciate that what is normal is not necessarily best.

Having introduced his readers to the superior perspective of the physiologist, he is now prepared to elaborate on his earlier teaching. What is to be feared most of all, we recall, is *not* the 'blond beast' lurking 'at the core of all noble races' (GM I: 11), but the prospect of its extinction. '*Our* greatest danger', we also recall, is the 'diminution and levelling of European humanity', which makes us *weary* of humankind itself (GM I: 12). Our weariness, we now learn, is the result of our proximity to the sick, who, simply by virtue of their sickness, conduct an involuntary assault on everyone and everything that is still healthy. Building on his earlier account of the corrosive power of *ressentiment* (GM I: 11), he now declares that 'the *sick* are humankind's greatest danger', for they threaten to dispossess us of 'our trust in life, in humankind, and in ourselves'. Contact with the sick therefore must be restricted to those who are appointed by life itself to tend to the sick.

He concludes this section by finally acknowledging his reliance on his readers. The 'good company' they share will help them, as a 'we', to guard against the twin contagions mentioned above: *nausea* and *pity*. Here he addresses his readers, for the first time, as his 'friends', and he suggests that these deadly contagions 'may be reserved' just for them. While he refrains from identifying their common destiny, he confirms the magnitude of its native perils. If the will to nothingness is produced by the union of nausea and pity, and if he and his friends are uniquely vulnerable to these contagions, then it is likely that the will to nothingness will arise, if at all, in and through *their* efforts. The task for which he recruits them is therefore pivotal: if they fail to avert the will to nothingness, they very well may serve as its unwitting hosts.

Section 15

Having established that the healthy must be segregated from the sick, Nietzsche now asserts 'the necessity of doctors and nurses *who are themselves sick*'. Life, he apparently means to claim, would neither abandon the sick to their suffering nor oblige the healthy to tend to them. This can only mean that life has designated certain sick individuals to care for other, sicker individuals, which in turn means that life itself supports a regimen of segregation and quarantine. The 'meaning of the ascetic priest' thus lies in his designated service to those who are sicker than he. Here we should note that Nietzsche and his friends are similarly obliged to endure prolonged contact with sickness, as they conduct their investigation of the ascetic priest. Whether or not they too qualify as ascetic priests remains to be seen.

Duly acknowledging the ascetic priest as 'the predestined savior, shepherd, and advocate of the sick herd', Nietzsche now turns to consider what it means that the ascetic priest is *also* sick. He promptly assigns the ascetic priest to a previously unknown hybrid category of animal taxonomy. This kind of animal is distinguished by its dominant expression of affect and, in turn, by its improbably successful approach to warcraft. While a war of *violence* clearly favours the martial physicality of the knightly nobles (GM I: 7), a war of *cunning* favours the inventive ingenuity of the priest. In particular, we now learn, the priest could transform *himself* into a 'new type' of beast of prey, who would promptly demonstrate why he is such a formidable adversary of all things healthy:

> He brings salves and balm with him, no doubt; but before he can act as a physician he first has to wound; when he then stills the pain of the wound *he at the same time infects the wound*—

According to this account, the priest 'evolved' into his deadliest incarnation in response to the provocations of those whom he later would target for domestication.

While the priest ably 'defends his sick herd' against the healthy and powerful, he displays his true genius in defending his herd against *itself*. The 'most dangerous' of the 'explosives' buried within the herd is its *ressentiment*, which, as a function of the herd's impotence, 'is constantly accumulating'. In order to prevent an explosion of *ressentiment* that would threaten to destroy 'herd and herdsman' alike, the priest arranges for the inward, rather than outward, discharge of *ressentiment*. Before his followers could embrace this ingenious alternative, however, they needed to arrive at the belief that *they* were their own worst enemies. How were they persuaded to take up, and act upon, such a patently false belief?

Anticipating his readers' need for further elaboration, Nietzsche resumes his physiological explanation of suffering. Returning to the scene described earlier in GM, he now expands upon his earlier account of how the miserable caged animal 'became the inventor of the "bad conscience" ' (GM II: 16). In doing so, he also demonstrates the superiority of his perspective to that of the priest, who both misunderstands and exploits the suffering of his herd. Building on his earlier discussions of suffering (cf. GM II: 7), Nietzsche reveals that

> Every sufferer instinctively seeks a cause for his suffering; more exactly, an agent;[95] still more specifically . . . a *guilty* agent . . . upon which he can, under some pretext or other, vent his affects, actually or in effigy: for the venting of his affects represents the greatest attempt on the part of the sufferer to win relief, *anesthesia* – the narcotic he cannot help desiring to deaden pain of any kind.

Nietzsche thus identifies the accumulation and expression of *ressentiment* as a natural (if crude) internal mechanism for anaesthetizing oneself. In seeking to discharge their copious *ressentiment*, that is, these sufferers had no reasonable expectation of actually prevailing over their healthy oppressors. They hoped simply to deaden their pain, and their oppressors furnished them with a proximate target for the discharge of *ressentiment* that would bring them relief.

In redirecting the *ressentiment* of his followers, the priest simply adjusted their natural mechanism for anaesthetizing themselves. Their inward discharge of *ressentiment* served the same purpose as their planned (but aborted) outward discharge, for it employed a 'violent emotion' to '*deaden* . . . a tormenting, secret pain that is becoming unendurable'. In making this adjustment, the priest also discovered that their need for anaesthesia was so great that it trumped even their fear of death. Until he intervened, after all, they were fully prepared to vent their *ressentiment* against their oppressors, despite knowing that any such discharge would be likely to provoke a fatal, retaliatory response. The priest thus realized that they would participate in their own annihilation if they could be convinced that doing so would relieve their suffering. This means, as he no doubt observed and filed away for future reference, that his sickly sufferers could easily be persuaded to engage their *will to nothingness*. As we shall see, this realization would eventually enable the priest to transform his ministry into a vehicle for his revenge.

Rather than deliver them from their death wish, which he was powerless to do in any event, the priest persuaded them to exchange their swift and certain death at the hands of their oppressors for the slow and certain death of self-annihilation – though he did not identify it as such. Aware that 'any pretext at all' would suffice to excite the 'savage' effects that would in turn provide the desired anaesthesia, the priest crafted a pretext – the bad conscience – that would relieve their suffering while also preventing them from agitating against their oppressors. This particular pretext furnished them with the perfect culprit: Each of them was the 'guilty agent' to blame for his own suffering! They suffered, that is, because they *deserved* to suffer. While this claim is 'brazen and false enough', it nevertheless achieved its intended aim: 'the direction of *ressentiment* [was] *altered*'.

Section 16

Flattering his readers once again, Nietzsche assumes that they can 'guess' what 'life has at least *attempted* through the ascetic priest'. His assumption that they are now familiar with the 'curative instinct of life' furthermore suggests that they, too, occupy (or at least appreciate) the superior perspective of the physiologist.

Through the ascetic priest, life attempted to provide the most tormented of human sufferers with a means of coping with their suffering and, perhaps, turning it to their advantage. By organizing these sufferers into a herd, wherein they could cultivate the habits conducive to 'self-discipline, self-surveillance, and self-overcoming', the ascetic priest succeeded in protecting them from others and from themselves. As it turns out, life never meant for the ascetic priest to serve as an actual physician. He is licensed to dispense only 'affect medication', which means that he 'cannot possibly bring about a real *cure* of sickness in a physiological sense'. In appointing the priest to minister to the sick, that is, life meant to create nothing more than a '*chasm* between healthy and sick', which served to establish a mutually beneficial regimen of segregation and quarantine.

Nietzsche closes this section by once again complimenting his readers. In a lengthy parenthesis, he reveals that he has proceeded throughout Essay III on the assumption that he need not demonstrate that human 'sinfulness' is simply an 'interpretation' of the more basic 'fact' of 'physiological depression'. This parenthesis thus marks the achievement of a significant milestone in the education of his readers, who no longer labour under the constraints of the dominant 'religio-moral' perspective. Owing to the progress of his readers, Nietzsche now may rely on the comparatively sophisticated diagnosis of *depression* as he completes his physiological-psychological profile of the ascetic priest.

Section 17

Nietzsche returns to his discussion of the ascetic priest by means of a rhetorical question: 'But is he really a *physician*?' In light of what he has just said about his readers, he cannot intend this question seriously. In fact, his aim in this section is to begin an audit of the priest's methods for treating depression, each of which 'combats only the suffering itself' and thus falls short of a genuine cure. The ascetic priest is not a physician, that is, because he fails to address the actual 'cause' of suffering, the 'real sickness'.

To prove his point, Nietzsche proceeds to adopt the 'religio-moral' perspective of the priest. From this perspective, he is able not only to express his genuine admiration for the 'genius' of the priest, but also to praise Christianity itself as a 'great treasure house of ingenious means of consolation'. Having granted the priest his due, Nietzsche next adopts a perspective that allows him to 'set bounds' to his admiration for the priest. He subsequently offers an alternative, physiological account of the kind of suffering the priest typically treats; this account is meant to demonstrate the inadequacy of the priest's methods of treatment.

Generalizing from the case at hand, Nietzsche traces the origins and enduring attraction of religion to the age-old struggle with 'a certain weariness and heaviness grown to epidemic proportions'. The periodic occurrence of such crises is certainly plausible, he believes, especially if they are understood to arise from the unchecked spread of a *'feeling of physiological inhibition'*. Rather than trace these crises to their true origins – e.g. the sudden 'mixing' of races and classes, the mismatching of races to climates, the introduction of inappropriate diets, or the onset of disease and conditions of degeneration – religion attributes them to the native defects of sinful souls.

Nietzsche's alternative explanation of the origin of this 'feeling of inhibition' is meant to expose the limits of the priest's powers of diagnosis and treatment. As it turns out, in fact, the ascetic priest commands access to only one perspective, whose narrow angle of vision restricts him to the occult causes of the 'psychological-moral domain'. As far as the priest knows, in fact, there simply is no 'cure', no 'salvation', apart from the 'mere affect medication' that he dispenses. This also means, as we have seen, that the priest is not a credible judge of the success of his ministry. For a more reliable evaluation of the priest, we must turn to someone who commands fluent access to multiple perspectives.

Before we do so, however, let us take note of Nietzsche's 'ability *to control* [his] Pro and Con and dispose of them' (GM III: 12),[96] which in turn attests to his achievement of 'objectivity' with respect to the ascetic priest. Rather than dismiss the 'religio-moral' perspective, he demonstrates instead that its relevance is and should be limited. Within the bounds of the 'psychological-moral domain', that is, the priest's perspective is valid and his 'curative' powers helpful. As we have seen, in fact, it was the priest's original diagnosis of the caged animal's self-inflicted suffering that launched humankind along the developmental arc that, even now, it continues to describe. In this domain, moreover, the physiological considerations that Nietzsche champions are not particularly pressing. Those to whom the priest is authorized to dispense his affect medication are in no position to envision for themselves the healthier existence that a physiological perspective discloses. The superiority of Nietzsche's physiological perspective therefore does not negate the limited value of the priest's 'religio-moral' perspective.

Having exposed the limitations of the priest's perspective, Nietzsche finally commences his physiological evaluation of the priest's methods for treating depression. As we might expect, the efficacy of these methods is limited by the priest's ignorance of the physiological basis of the condition he proposes to cure. The priest's first method of combating depression involves his attempt to 'reduce the feeling of life in general to its lowest point'. While the priest and his followers describe this method in terms of the pursuit and realization of a 'selfless' existence, undisturbed by will, desire and affect, the physiological truth of the matter is that this method aims to sustain 'the minimum metabolism at which life will still subsist without really entering consciousness'. This method thus produces a condition that closely approximates *not willing*, which, as we have seen, is intolerable to the human will in its current, post-instinctual form (GM III: 1).

With respect to this particular method, the priest is essentially a hypnotist, for he simply wishes to produce in his disciples a trance-like condition in which they can remain permanently dissociated from the feelings, cravings and affects that are likely to connect them to their depression. It is this condition, Nietzsche believes, that mystics and ascetics mistakenly identify as 'the supreme state, *redemption* itself'.

Section 18

As it turns out, however, the method discussed in the previous section is only rarely employed. It 'presupposes rare energy', which most sickly individuals do not possess. A far more common method of treating depression involves an immersion in *'mechanical activity'*, which diverts the sufferer's attention away from himself and thereby prevents the feeling of pain from entering consciousness. Nietzsche compliments the priest for his 'ingenuity' in helping sufferers to appreciate the blessings and virtues of work that they otherwise would find unrewarding or demeaning. Under the proper description, that is, just about any form of labour can be tolerated and even embraced, provided it distracts the workers from their suffering.

A third method of combating depression involves the priest in 'the prescribing of a *petty pleasure* that is easily attainable and can be made into a regular event'. Most commonly, the priest prescribes the 'pleasure of *giving* [or making] pleasure', which in turn promotes the

excitement of the strongest, most life-affirming drive, even if in the most cautious doses – namely, of the *will to power*.

Here Nietzsche exposes the physiological truth underlying charity, pity, alms-giving and all other social expressions of altruism: helping others affords even the sickliest human beings an opportunity to cultivate the naturally desirable feeling of 'slight superiority' over others. By prescribing acts and routines that promote this feeling, the priest defers indefinitely the more overt expressions of cruelty that his sufferers would otherwise be obliged to direct toward one another. The prescribing of petty pleasures also contributes to the 'awakening of the communal feeling of power', which distracts the individual from his own suffering by promoting his identification with the 'prosperity of the community' (GM III: 19). It is by means of this third method that the individual acquires a sense of identity that is positively related to the creation and expansion of the herd.[97]

Returning to the 'beginnings of Christianity in the Roman world', Nietzsche discovers widespread 'conscious employment' of this method for treating depression. Adding welcome detail to his earlier account of the slave revolt in morality, he identifies 'the formation of a herd [as] a significant victory and advance in the struggle against depression'. Had Christianity remained primarily concerned to care for sufferers and treat their depression, in fact, it might have played an enduring, constructive role within the lowest strata of the Roman Empire. But the ascetic priest did not remain content for long in this limited role. As we have seen, he discerned in the creation of the herd a unique opportunity to pursue his own interests, which only appeared to coincide with those of the herd. Able to manipulate the will to power of the sufferers entrusted to his care, the priest set his sights on revenge.

Nietzsche thus implies that this third method of treating depression naturally led to the development of the notorious fourth method, to which he now turns.

Section 19

Here Nietzsche shifts his focus from the priest's 'innocent' methods of combating depression to his 'guilty' methods. This shift marks an important development in his profile of the priestly type, for this distinction is available to him only by virtue of the physiological perspective he now commands. He thus claims to see what the priest cannot – namely, that the priest's methods become 'guilty' when they exacerbate the suffering of those whom he treats. Here it becomes clear, in fact, that the ascetic priest actually creates in his victims the need – the more accurate physiological term might be *addiction* – to which he subsequently responds.

This shift in focus also corresponds to a narrowing of Nietzsche's psychological-physiological profile of the ascetic priest. Although he continues to refer, simply, to the ascetic priest, he actually has in mind a specific historical individual: the apostle Paul, to whom he attributes this pivotal expansion of the priestly mission.[98] According to Nietzsche, it was Paul who discovered how to mobilize the herd against the barbaric 'nations' of the Empire, whose health and good conscience he resented.[99] Paul favoured the priest's 'guilty' methods of combating suffering, that is, because they also allowed him to pursue his personal agenda of revenge. Nietzsche's examination of the ascetic priest's 'guilty' methods, which comprises Sections 19–21, thus presupposes as its historical context the founding of Christianity, which Nietzsche traces not to the omni-affirmative teachings of Christ, but to the vengeful teachings of Paul.

Here Nietzsche describes himself and his readers as versed in *psychology* as well as *physiology*.[100] While he regards these two sciences as intimately related, the former is especially pertinent to the immediate task at hand. Having corrected the long-standing 'psychological misunderstanding' of the ascetic ideal (GM III: 13), he now confronts a more formidable obstacle to the completion of his profile of the ascetic priest. In order to explore the priest's 'more interesting' methods in the struggle against depression, he and his readers must now expose – and endure – the 'innocence' with which 'modern souls' lie about themselves and their motives. He thus cautions his readers to beware the 'great danger' that lies ahead – namely, the 'great nausea' that could tempt them to abandon their quest. (As we have seen, their susceptibility to this particular danger is a product of their unprecedented exposure to 'the sickening fumes of inner corruption and the hidden rot of disease' (GM II: 14).) The urgency of this word of caution thus becomes apparent, for they are about to confront the sickening physiological truth of morality itself: the so-called 'good' individual, whose care and veneration have exhausted the cultural resources of European civilization itself, is in fact a decadent.[101]

In what initially appears to be a digression from his main narrative, Nietzsche launches an extended rant against 'modern books' and the 'good men' who write them. These 'good men' are so thoroughly moralized that they are unable to tell the 'honest' lies that he claims to prefer. He concludes that a 'prudent man' would be foolhardy to 'write a single honest word about himself today'. The relevance of this apparent digression thus becomes clear: Nietzsche is preparing to say an 'honest word' or two about himself (and his readers) – in a 'modern book', no less – and he acknowledges in advance that he may be 'foolish' to do so. But he is not deterred.

This section thus marks the achievement of an important, if precarious, milestone in the training of his readers. As psychologists, they are finally prepared to investigate the means employed by the priest to orchestrate orgies of feeling in those sinners who seek the anaesthesia he has taught them to crave. Their investigation thus requires them to turn *inward*, and to describe as honestly as possible the physiological preconditions and effects of the priest's ministrations. In doing so, they are likely to encounter instances of 'moralistic mendaciousness' within themselves, which may stall or impede their investigation. In particular, they may not yet be prepared to face the truth of their own involvement in – much less their enjoyment of – the priest's 'guilty' methods for treating depression.

This point is well taken, for the all-too-human truth about these orgies of feeling is not particularly flattering either to the priest or to those in whom they are orchestrated. As we shall see, in fact, the secret of the priest's success is that his 'guilty' methods excite in his followers a *will to nothingness*, i.e. a will to destroy the conditions of their very existence. What Nietzsche and his fellow psychologists are reluctant to admit, presumably, is that the will to nothingness is both native to all human beings *and* all-too-easy to arouse. This means, among other things, that the victims of priestly mischief only rarely see themselves as such. They fervently crave the 'orgies of feeling' that the priest is able to excite in them, and they are eternally grateful to him for satisfying their craving. If Nietzsche is to make his case against the priest, that is, he will not be able to count on the testimony of those whom the priest has ruined.

Section 20

The relevance of the 'moral' proposed in the previous section becomes immediately evident. Nietzsche volunteers that he and his fellow psychologists are 'unable to shake off a certain mistrust of [*them*]*selves*'. Perhaps they, too, need to find something unqualifiedly *good* in human nature, some unshakable attachment to life that would blunt the allure of a self-consuming explosion of affect. Perhaps they, too, need to pretend that the will to nothingness arises, if at all, only in the most extreme cases of psychopathology. If so, their investigation will go awry and the psychology of the ascetic priest will remain a mystery.

At this point, Nietzsche's conscience asserts itself once again; as before, moreover, it propels him forward. Whether prudently or foolishly (or both), he now applies to himself his evaluation in the previous section of 'modern books' and the 'good men' who write and read them. In a remarkable gesture of self-disclosure,[102] he freely admits that he and his readers are probably 'too good' for the task of undertaking a psychological investigation of the ascetic priest's 'guilty' methods for combating depression.[103] In particular, they may be 'too good' to acknowledge the pull of their own Dionysian urges toward self-destruction and self-dissolution, of which these 'orgies of feeling' provide an appetizing foretaste. In any event, this gesture of self-disclosure also serves to distinguish Nietzsche from the ascetic priest, who, as we have seen, acknowledges no limitations either to his perspective or to his ministry.

Returning the focus of his narrative to 'our problem', Nietzsche announces his intention to fill another gap in his main narrative. Now apprised of the physiological basis of depression, we are finally prepared to learn how the caged animal described in Essay II was instructed – on two separate occasions – in the treatment of its self-inflicted suffering. Here Nietzsche confirms that the pain of the bad conscience can be deadened only by a diversionary 'explosion' of powerful affects, which in turn produces the 'orgy of feeling' that is the priest's signature form of medication. As we have seen, of course, this medication provides only temporary relief. Once its diversionary effects subside, the caged animal is even sicker than before and in need of ever stronger explosions of affect. This method is 'guilty', that is, because it *compounds* the physical suffering of those to whom it is prescribed.[104]

The priest's 'guilty' method of combating depression thus trades on an ingenious 'exploitation' of the bad conscience. As we have seen, the priest initially intervened to treat the caged animal for the self-inflicted suffering that attends the inward discharge of instinctual aggression (GM II: 16). Confronted with 'the feeling of guilt in its raw state', the priest was powerless to diagnose this feeling, much less to eliminate it. Instead, drawing on his own experience of self-loathing and self-recrimination,[105] the priest urged the caged animal to search within himself for the cause of his suffering. The priest thus offered the caged animal a justification for his suffering – namely, as a well-deserved *punishment* for his misdeeds and broken promises – and developed an effective method for combating its symptoms. Duly diagnosed as the *bad conscience*, the self-inflicted suffering that had driven the caged animal to contemplate suicide became a source of inspiration and enhanced vitality. With the help of the priest, that is, the caged animal learned to take joy once again in the venting of his animal aggression, even though he was also the target of this discharge. Supplemented by the distractions endemic to herd life – e.g. mutual aid, misery-loving company, exhausting mechanical labour, transient experiences of slight superiority, and so on – this acquired taste for suffering provided the caged animal with an effective justification of his otherwise miserable existence.

With the dawning of Christianity, we learned (GM II: 22), the caged animal abandoned this 'innocent' method of treatment in favour of a method that we now know to be 'guilty'. We are now in a position to understand that the priest intervened for a second time, offering to treat the caged animal with a more potent form of affect medication. Resorting once again to the only trick he knows, the priest convinced the caged animal to turn inward. This time around, the caged animal discovered that his debts were so great as to be irremediable. No longer merely a *debtor*, he knew himself to be a *sinner*. He was persuaded to this discovery, we now understand, by the breathtaking prospect of *unlimited* punishment, from which he would receive regular, ever-escalating doses of the anaesthesia he craved. With the help of the priest, that is, the caged animal developed a craving for the consciousness-blotting orgies of feeling that are available only to the most depraved of sinners. Here we witness the installation of a second, amplified version of the ascetic ideal.

By implicating the priest in the historical production of the *sinner*, Nietzsche encourages us to connect the seemingly disjointed narratives of Essays I and II. Indeed, his reference to the dawning of Christianity confirms what we have suspected all along: the creative genius behind the slave revolt in morality was none other than the ascetic priest. It was he who impregnated the *ressentiment* of the slaves, such that they eventually came to equate *goodness* with suffering and *evil* with nobility (GM I: 10). As we now know, moreover, the slave revolt reached its fruition in the first century CE under the creative genius of a specific ascetic priest: the apostle Paul. His unique contribution was to provide a new, intensified diagnosis of the suffering that tormented the caged animal described in Essay II. With a single stroke, that is, Paul transformed slaves, sufferers and debtors alike into guilty *sinners*.

This reference to the dawning of Christianity also allows Nietzsche to direct our attention, finally, to the *real* damage done by the ascetic priest. As we have seen, the priest's relationship to the ascetic ideal is predicated in part on its *utility*, as an 'instrument of . . . [and] license for power' (GM III: 1). The priest's desire for power in fact explains how and why he developed a special affinity for his 'guilty' method of treating depression. While all of his methods of treatment provide his followers with temporary relief from pain, his 'guilty' method also allows him to extend the reach of his ministry. His reliance on this method not only cultivates in his followers a relationship of escalating dependency, but also deputizes them to recruit new disciples. Nietzsche thus concludes this section by wondering, rhetorically, if the priest is still entitled to repeat Jesus' claim that his 'kingdom is not of *this* world'. If the priest is not so entitled, then something else, something unmistakably *this*-worldly, must be going on with his ministry.

Section 21

Nietzsche begins this section by rhetorically addressing anyone who believes that the priest's 'guilty' method of treating depression has actually '*benefited*' those to whom it has been prescribed. He is willing to grant that some human beings have been '*improved*' by this method, but only if 'improvement' is understood to involve *taming*, *weakening*, and so forth.[106]

Nietzsche's gibe marks an important shift in the focus of his narrative. Thus far, he has been content to document the harm done by the priest to the sickly sufferers entrusted to his care. As he has shown (and here confirms), the priest's 'guilty' method of treating depression invariably makes the sick sicker. If he is to make his larger case against the ascetic ideal, however, he now must demonstrate that this method is more generally ruinous. In this passage, he thus identifies, albeit implicitly, the true victims of the priest's power grab: the healthy, fortunate, beast-of-prey human beings who are 'tamed', 'weakened' and 'emasculated' in the process.[107] (That he is not speaking here of the 'sick, distressed and depressed' becomes clear when he turns explicitly in the next sentence to consider their plight.) The priest became truly dangerous, and his ministry generally ruinous, when he expanded his clientele to include those strong, barbaric individuals whom he would need to *tame* in order to *improve*, and to *sicken* in order to *tame*.

History furthermore reveals that 'wherever the ascetic priest has prevailed with this treatment, sickness has spread in depth *and breadth* with astonishing speed' (emphasis added). This can only mean that the priest's 'guilty' method for combating depression both exacerbates the torment of those who already suffer *and creates new sufferers*, whom he might subsequently treat. As we have seen, the key to his assimilation of new sufferers into his herd is his indiscriminate teaching of *pity*, through which he pledges his allegiance to *all* sufferers, including those who by all rights should be allowed (and even encouraged) to die. By promoting an 'ever spreading morality of pity' (GM P5), that is, the priest ensured that his ministry would become increasingly indispensable to an ever-expanding clientele of sinners. As we are now in a position to understand, in fact, the priest's acquired preference for this 'guilty' method of treating depression bears witness to the ascendancy of his personal agenda, which he has indirectly pursued through his ministry to the sick.

The priest's personal agenda is apparently an outgrowth of his archaic hatred, grown to 'monstrous and uncanny proportions' (GM I: 7), of his enemies. Rather than attack his enemies directly, however, the priest dispatches his army of sinners to destroy the material and social conditions of the noble way of life. Having discovered by chance his improbable power over the noble beasts of prey (GM III: 15), he exemplifies his disciples to poison the good conscience of anyone who employs the noble mode of valuation.[108] He seeks to extend his secular dominion, that is, not simply to accumulate power for its own sake, or to recruit more company for the misery of his followers, but to gain revenge against the healthy, noble, masterly types whose happiness and good fortune he resents. The 'sickly sheep' he has ruined in the process are merely collateral damage in his war of cunning against the healthy.

At this point, we would do well to acknowledge once again the unidentified historical context of Nietzsche's profile of the ascetic priest. As we have seen, it was Paul who came to favour the 'guilty' method of combating depression, and it was Paul who first used this method to treat (= tame) barbarians and beasts of prey. In gaining his revenge against the despised 'nations', that is, Paul masterminded the eventual victory of 'Judea' over 'Rome':

> What [Paul] guessed was how one could use the little sectarian Christian movement apart from Judaism to kindle a 'world fire'; how with the symbol of 'God on the cross' one could unite all who lay at the bottom . . . into a tremendous power. (A 58)

As this passage suggests, Nietzsche's enmity for Paul may have been so great that he elected not to name his opponent in GM. Determined to wage war only in the event that 'every personal quarrel is excluded', so that an 'attack is . . . a proof of good will, sometimes even of gratitude' (EH: 'wise' 7), he may have had no choice in GM but to focus more generally on the nameless, faceless ascetic priest.

Throughout Essay III, in fact, Nietzsche has been careful not to *blame* the ascetic priest for the destructive effects of the ascetic ideal.

His primary objective in Sections 17–21 has been to show that, and why, the ascetic priest cannot be considered a genuine physician. Appointed solely to protect the sickly sufferers entrusted to his care, the priest cannot be expected to protect the rich diversity of human types, much less those higher types whose exotic health he resents. Nietzsche thus explains that the ascetic priest conducts his ministry '*with a good conscience*', prescribes his guilty method with 'the profoundest faith in its utility', and suffers personally from 'the misery he has caused' (GM III: 20). Assigned to protect declining forms of life, the priest cannot possibly imagine that life also acts to *limit* his conservatory efforts, especially when the declining forms that he preserves threaten to degrade the overall diversity of life.[109] Through no fault of his own, that is, the priest does not acknowledge, much less honour, the higher interests of life. He cannot be considered a genuine physician, for life neither intended nor trained him to serve in this capacity. This also means, as we shall see, that he cannot be expected to hear, much less heed, life's call to surrender himself to the law of self-overcoming.

We should not be surprised to learn, then, that the priest attempts the *opposite* of what the physician is obliged to accomplish.[110] In seeking revenge against his enemies, the priest preserves sickly, degenerating human beings precisely in order to crowd out the healthier types whom he resents. As Nietzsche explains elsewhere, this pathological commitment to the preservation of the 'incurable' – known in the vernacular as *pity* – is what distinguishes the priest most decisively from the physiologist:

> The physiologist demands *excision* of the degenerating part; he denies all solidarity with what degenerates; he is worlds removed from pity for it. But the priest desires precisely the degeneration of the whole, of humanity: for that reason, he *conserves* what degenerates – at this price he rules. (EH 'dawn' 2)[111]

This passage also illuminates Nietzsche's likely strategy for distinguishing himself once and for all from the ascetic priest. As we have seen, he regards himself as both an opponent of the ascetic priest and as a physiologist. Although GM contains no explicit 'demands' for the 'excision of the degenerating part' of humankind, the task to which he will soon invite his readers requires them to affirm the excision of all that remains of Christian morality. In the sections of GM to follow, in fact, Nietzsche presents himself as both a physiologist *and* a physician, for he actually volunteers to *perform* the excision that he demands. As we shall see, his true test as a physician is also the true test of his individuation from the ascetic priest. In the end, he must turn the healing scalpel on *himself*, excising the residual will to truth that sustains his intellectual conscience.

Having concluded his physiological and psychological investigations of the ascetic priest, Nietzsche pronounces his indictment of the ascetic ideal:

> I know of hardly anything else that has had so destructive an effect upon the *health* and racial strength of Europeans as this ideal; one may without any exaggeration call it *the true calamity* in the history of European health.

This pronouncement raises the stakes of the discussion to follow, for it asserts that the ascetic ideal has been far more harmful than even its harshest critics have dared to suppose. Having demonstrated the superiority of his physiological perspective, Nietzsche now must prove that he is also a physician. This he can accomplish only by excising the degeneration that threatens the rich diversity of life.

Section 22

Ostensibly finished with the ascetic priest, Nietzsche digresses a bit,[112] alleging that the ascetic priest 'has also ruined *taste* in *artibus et litteris*'. His case in point is the Christian New Testament, whose reception thus far encourages him to contrast his 'singular' taste with the 'ruined' taste that has defined the past 'two millennia'. In developing this particular criticism of the ascetic ideal, he is apparently able to set aside his earlier doubts about his own 'good taste' (GM III: 19).

Here Nietzsche stands, like Luther at Worms, unable to do otherwise. He has 'the courage of his bad taste', which, of course, he does not regard as *bad* at all – especially when compared to the 'loutish' taste of the 'peasant' Luther, who insisted that he deserved 'to speak directly . . . with his God'. Here Nietzsche intimates that the ascetic ideal has in fact encouraged in Christians a vanity beyond comparison. As the example of Luther is meant to confirm, Christians feel entitled not only to pronounce the name of their deity, but also to carry on with their deity in an extremely informal manner, as if their God had nothing better to do than hear the petty complaints of every disgruntled peasant.

Nietzsche concludes from the case of Luther that 'the ascetic ideal has never and nowhere been a school of good taste, even less of good manners'. This is so, as he explains, because the ascetic ideal expresses a 'dislike of moderation', and is a *'non plus ultra'*. (As we have seen, the ascetic priest acknowledges no limits to his sphere of jurisdiction and in fact refuses to countenance any distinction between those who would and would not benefit from his ministry.) This is why Nietzsche has attempted to cultivate in his readers the virtues of deference, restraint, silence, patience and, above all, good taste. Their possession of these virtues will facilitate their efforts to distinguish themselves from the ascetic priest.

Section 23
Rather than continue to enumerate the many things that the ascetic ideal has ruined, Nietzsche reminds himself and his readers that the 'purpose' of Essay III is 'to bring to light, not what this ideal has *done*, but simply what it *means*'. He subsequently poses a series of rhetorical questions that are meant to illuminate the meaning of the ascetic ideal at its deepest, and most terrifying, layer of significance:

> What is the meaning of the *power* of this ideal, the monstrous nature of its power? Why has it been allowed to flourish to this extent? Why has it not rather been resisted? The ascetic ideal expresses a will: *Where* is the opposing will that might express an *opposing ideal*? (GM III: 23)

Especially at first glance, it might appear that Nietzsche has already answered these questions. The will expressed by the ascetic ideal is embodied by the ascetic priest, whose '*right* to exist stands or falls with that ideal' (GM III: 11). Presumably, then, the opposing will, which will express an opposing ideal, will be embodied by the new philosopher, whose triumphant debut was foretold in Section 10. The ascetic ideal has not yet met its match, that is, because the new philosopher has not yet emancipated himself from the patronage of the ascetic priest. As the new philosopher establishes for himself a fully individuated existence, he will muster the opposing will that expresses an opposing ideal. Until that time, however, we should not expect to encounter a viable alternative to the ascetic ideal.

This last point suggests another line of interpretation. In posing these rhetorical questions, Nietzsche hopes to guide his best readers toward the realization that they are mistaken about the nature of their opposition to the ascetic ideal.[113] The indirect communication he initiates in this section is thus meant to persuade his readers of three points: 1) as scholars, they oppose the ascetic ideal not in the sense of providing or promoting an alternative ideal, but in the sense of turning the power of the ascetic ideal against itself;[114] 2) their opposition thus far has succeeded in eliminating only what is already lifeless and obsolete in the ascetic ideal; and 3) although their opposition thus far has not damaged the ascetic ideal, they are historically positioned to facilitate (and perhaps hasten) its demise. They may do so, as we shall see, by opposing the ascetic ideal as it is expressed and embodied *in them*. In order to do so, however, they first must recognize themselves as champions of the ascetic ideal.

Immediately after posing these rhetorical questions, Nietzsche turns to consider the claim that *science* (i.e. scholarly inquiry) expresses an alternative to the ascetic ideal. The choice of science is by no means arbitrary. Those readers who make up his target audience are likely not only to regard themselves as scientists (or scholars), but also to understand their scholarly activity as inimical to the ascetic ideal. While they are not incorrect to regard science as the natural opponent of the ascetic ideal, they fail as yet to appreciate the unique historical significance of their own scholarly activity. He thus informs them that

> Science today . . . is not the opposite of the ascetic ideal but rather *the latest and noblest form of it*. Does that sound strange to you?

The assertion of this claim marks an important development in Nietzsche's investigation of the ascetic ideal. He will proceed to show that the authority of the ascetic ideal has declined to the point that it now motivates only those scholars who retain their faith in the saving power of truth. More importantly, he will attempt to convince his readers that, as strange as it may sound, *they* are the ascetic scholars to whom he refers in this passage.

He begins this process by presenting his readers with what appears to be a stark either/or. Having asserted that some scholars conduct an ascetic search for truth, he concedes that most scholars pursue their research without the benefit of a guiding ideal, goal, will or faith. With this latter group in mind, he observes that 'science today is a *hiding place* for every kind of discontent, disbelief, gnawing worm, *despectio sui*, [and] bad conscience'. This approach to science 'conceals' from observers and scholars alike that it now serves its practitioners 'as a means of self-narcosis'. The implication here is that his readers, scholars in their own right, belong either with the unwitting champions of the ascetic ideal or with those '*sufferers* . . . who fear only one thing: *regaining consciousness*'. As strange as the former position may seem to them, it is certainly preferable to the notion that they lead at best a semi-conscious existence.

Section 24

Nietzsche now turns to consider the 'rare exceptions' that he mentioned in the previous section. Even if we agree that mainstream science does not oppose the ascetic ideal, is it not possible that the 'rarer cases' among scholars are able to do so? In particular, he wonders if 'the last idealists left among philosophers and scholars' might be the 'desired *opponents* of the ascetic ideal, the counter-idealists?' That *they* believe this to be the case is clear enough from the 'seriousness' and 'passion' with which they proclaim their opposition to the ascetic ideal. Although they are not incorrect to regard themselves as 'counter-idealists', they labour under the misconception that the target of their opposition, the ascetic ideal, is external and unrelated to them. They will realize their destiny as opponents of the ascetic ideal only in the event that they resolve to oppose *themselves*, for they are the last remaining champions of the ascetic ideal.

At this point, Nietzsche once again presumes to speak on behalf of his target audience. 'We "knowers",' he asserts, 'have gradually come to mistrust believers of all kinds', for strong belief typically attests to the likelihood of self-deception on the part of the believers. He thus asks his readers if this is true as well of those 'last idealists' who fancy themselves opponents of the ascetic ideal. In order to appreciate the rhetorical thrust of this question, let us note that his reference here to *mistrust* recalls the opening sentences of Section 20, where he conceded that he and his best readers are probably 'too good' to conduct the honest psychological inquiry that is required of them. At that point, of course, their mistrust was explicitly identified as directed at *themselves*. At this point, their mistrust is once again directed at themselves, even though it is not identified as such, for *they* are the 'last idealists' to whom he refers in this section. Nietzsche and his fellow 'knowers' thus belong *among* those believers whom they have already come with good reason to mistrust. This means, of course, that they should eventually extend their mistrust to themselves, which is precisely what Nietzsche means for them to do.

Having held up a mirror for his readers, he now must help them to see themselves in the image it reflects. This is no easy task, however, for he needs them to recognize themselves under the aspect that they are most likely to reject out of hand – namely, as believers, as knights of *faith*. In an attempt to guide his best readers toward the realization that they are the 'last idealists' described in this section, he now implements two strategies of indirection.[115] His first strategy is to describe these 'last idealists' as if they were a third party (or 'they'), while also emphasizing their affinities with himself and his 'we'. His ensuing description of these 'last idealists' thus ascribes to them virtues, attributes and accomplishments that he also assigns to himself and his fellow 'knowers'.[116] As he readily concedes, moreover, he 'know[s] all this from too close up perhaps', which suggests an intimate, personal acquaintance with those who *claim*, mistakenly, to be free spirits.[117] Still, he stops just short of ascribing to his readers the residual faithfulness of these 'last idealists'. Throughout this section, in fact, he conspicuously neglects to avow his own allegiance to the ascetic ideal, even though, as we shall see, he freely does so elsewhere.

These 'last idealists' are not yet free spirits, he explains, because their 'unconditional will to truth' betrays their 'faith in a *metaphysical* value, *the absolute value of truth*'. His argument here is a bit compressed, but he apparently means to claim that: (1) in so far as idealism informs and motivates the practice of science, it does so on the strength of a *will to truth*, which (2) rests on an unacknowledged *faith in truth*, which in turn (3) takes the value of truth to be *absolute*, which (4) is a *metaphysical* value, which (5) presupposes the validity of the *ascetic ideal*. Were it not for their unacknowledged allegiance to the ascetic ideal, in fact, these 'last idealists' would be indistinguishable from those 'modest and worthy laborers' who pursue scientific research as a means of preventing themselves from 'regaining consciousness' (GM III: 23).

In support of this analysis, Nietzsche cites at length from GS 344, which bears the eye-opening title, *How we, too, are still pious.* Launching a second, complementary strategy of indirection, he relies on passages imported from GS to convey truths and insights that he is not yet willing to convey directly to the readers of GM. Whereas the text that is original to GM stops short of identifying Nietzsche and his 'we' with the 'last idealists' described in this section, the text imported from GS 344 leaves no doubt that he and his fellow 'knowers' are fully implicated in the faith in truth that characterizes the 'last idealists'. This strategy is apparently meant to remind his devoted readers of what they already (should) know from reading GS 344, and to encourage them to apply these recovered insights to themselves. He thus writes, for the second time, that

> [W]e knowers of today, we godless ones and anti-metaphysicians, we, too, still derive *our* flame from the fire ignited by a faith mil-lennia old . . . that truth is *divine.*

Especially when considered within the larger contexts that Nietzsche recommends to his readers (namely, GS 344, the whole of Book V of GS, and the 1886 Preface to *The Dawn*), this extract identifies him and his fellow 'knowers' as the 'last idealists' described in this section.

Finding it 'necessary to pause and take careful stock', Nietzsche ventures an answer to the question with which the extracted passage concludes. 'If God himself turns out be our *longest lie,*' he asks, are we not obliged to expose the kindred lie that supports our scientific and scholarly pursuits? If we wish to continue the progress marked by our renunciation of belief in the Christian God, that is, we will need to interrogate our allegiance to the successor deity. Having earlier alerted his readers to the affinities they share with the 'last idealists', Nietzsche here announces the *task* that separates his best readers from all other idealists:

> From the moment faith in the God of the ascetic ideal is denied, *a new problem arises*: that of the *value* of truth. The will to truth requires a critique – let us thus define our own task – the value of truth must for once be experimentally[118] *called into question.*

The dawning of this new problem thus brings the narrative of GM up to date, as the genealogist of morals becomes the central focus of his genealogy of morals. For the remainder of GM, in fact, Nietzsche finds himself in the awkward, and occasionally amusing, position of attempting to conclude an inquiry that is in fact extended by his every effort to bring it to a close. Having wandered onstage, he now finds himself no longer simply recording the history of European morality, but producing it as well.

As this passage indicates, Nietzsche hopes to persuade his fellow 'knowers' of the advantages that accrue to them as the final champions of the ascetic ideal. He thus reveals that he and they stand in a unique, dual relationship to the will to truth. As true believers, they are not free to renounce their faith in the saving power of truth. Inasmuch as they possess disposable reserves of strength, however, they may employ their will to truth in the service of a *critique* of the will to truth. Unlike lesser idealists, that is, they may venture to tell the truth about truth. Their critique must proceed 'experimentally', of course, for any question they raise about the value of truth must invariably derive its authority from the 'absolute value' they attach, involuntarily, to truth itself. As we shall see, in fact, the truth about truth may be fatally complicated.

There is another, more uniquely Nietzschean sense in which this critique of truth must proceed *experimentally*. If Nietzsche and his fellow 'knowers' are among the last believers in the divinity of truth, they will have little choice but to direct their critique of truth against *themselves*. (Even if they begin this critique by directing it toward others, as Nietzsche pretends to do in this section, they eventually must call into question their own unscientific estimations of the value of truth.) An 'experimental' critique of truth would thus require them to engage in *self-directed* criticism, the practice of which Nietzsche increasingly comes to recommend as a sign of renewed strength and renascent health. As we shall see, in fact, the requirement of self-directed criticism is central to his anticipated contribution to the destruction of Christian morality.

Section 25

Nietzsche begins this section by warning his readers not to give him the kind of answer that others have provided to the question he posed in Section 23. Science, he reiterates, is not the 'natural antagonist' of the ascetic ideal, and it may even 'be said to represent the driving force in its inner development'. Building on his earlier analysis of the ascetic ideal, he now insists that science 'attacks' only the 'exteriors' of the ascetic ideal, removing only its inessential 'guise and masquerade'. Here we should note, however, that Nietzsche runs a substantial risk in seeming to dismiss science (or scholarly research) as a source of opposition to the ascetic ideal. Although science is not currently antagonistic to the living core of the ascetic ideal, it may yet become so, especially if it is steered into opposition to the ascetic ideal by those scholars who would dare to conduct an experimental critique of the will to truth.

What champions of science have mistakenly identified thus far as their antagonism to the ascetic ideal has in fact contributed to its distillation and refinement. By stripping away the lifeless husk that surrounds the ascetic ideal in its condition of diminished authority, scholars have actually succeeded in isolating – and 'liberating' – its vital core. Attending once again to the training of his readers' senses, Nietzsche urges them to 'keep [their] eyes and ears open to [the] fact' that science and the ascetic ideal 'are *necessarily* allies'. This means, of course, that any credible challenge to the ascetic ideal also must address itself to science, and vice versa, for 'they can only be fought and called in question together'.

The basis for this alliance is worth noting, especially inasmuch as Nietzsche hopes to persuade his best readers to join him in a self-directed (and perhaps self-consuming) assault on these allies:

This pair, science and the ascetic ideal, both rest on . . . the same belief that truth is inestimable and cannot be criticized . . .

Nietzsche's point here is that the 'last idealists' draw their vitality and motivation from an unacknowledged faith in the saving power of truth. Rather than determine scientifically the value of truth, they simply assume, as a matter of faith, that the pursuit and possession of truth are invaluable. Their faith in truth in turn authorizes the disciplines of self-deprivation that structure the practice of their research, as well as the self-demeaning objectives that guide their scholarship. Their faith in truth thus betrays the deeper conviction that they stand in *need* of truth. Nothing short of its single-minded pursuit will redeem their faulted nature.

To support his point, Nietzsche observes that ever since Copernicus removed the earth from its presumed place at the centre of the cosmos, scientific advances have endeavoured to 'dissuad[e] humankind from its former respect for itself'. Echoing his earlier judgement of the self-loathing English psychologists (GM I: 1), he insists that scientific progress in the modern age bears witness to the secret motivation of the ascetic ideal. As we shall see, however, he also hopes to capitalize on this misanthropic trend in scientific research. The task to which he invites his best readers will involve them in a campaign to discredit the authority of the will to truth, which is also the basis for the 'intellectual conscience' that most notably identifies them as heirs to a noble lineage.

Section 26
Having demolished the claim that science (as yet) opposes the ascetic ideal, Nietzsche now inquires after the status of modern historiography. This inquiry furnishes the pretext for his tirade against the sham idealism of the 'contemplative historians', which he subsequently expands to include all others, including the anti-Semites, who promote bogus ideals.

Section 27
Relegating these sham idealists to 'yesterday and today', Nietzsche returns the focus of his narrative to '*our* problem, the problem of the *meaning* of the ascetic ideal', which uniquely pertains to the *future* of humankind. Recalling his earlier account of the alliance between science and the ascetic ideal (GM III: 25), he now identifies the *will to truth* as the unadulterated 'kernel' of the ascetic ideal. His implication here is that the cumulative opposition of scientists and scholars has stripped the ascetic ideal to its living core, which we are now in a position to identify as the will to truth. This means, of course, that aspiring opponents of the ascetic ideal must now direct their opposition against its animating will to truth, which they have no choice but to do as champions of the will to truth. In the end, that is, science may yet oppose the ascetic ideal, but only if those scholars who make up Nietzsche's target audience are willing to mount a self-directed critique of the will to truth.

Thus we see that the 'opposing will' that Nietzsche has pretended to seek in Sections 23–26 is none other than the will to truth. The 'opposing ideal' that the will to truth expresses is neither an alternative to the ascetic ideal nor exclusive of it, but is in fact the ascetic ideal in its purest, most concentrated form. In this form, which is unique to the epoch of late modernity, the ascetic ideal is indistinguishable from the scholarly quest for truth. Both find their justification in the pursuit of the same 'one goal' – namely, truth itself – which, supposedly, will redeem the faulted nature of the human condition. In the will to truth, the ascetic ideal finally has met its 'match', for the will to truth too

> permits no other interpretation, no other goal . . . it submits to no power, believes in its own predominance over every other power, in its absolute *superiority of rank* over every other power— (GM III: 23)

As it turns out, then, 'the desired *opponents* of the ascetic ideal, the *counteridealists*' (GM III: 24) are none other than Nietzsche and his fellow 'knowers' – provided, of course, that they now steer their will to truth into opposition with itself. Their task, in short, is to tell the truth about truth, which is precisely what champions of science have failed thus far to do. If successful in performing this task, as we shall see, they will hasten the destruction of Christian morality.

Nietzsche thus confirms that 'unconditional honest atheism' should not be considered the 'antithesis' of the ascetic ideal. Although practised by the 'more spiritual individuals of this age', atheism trades on the will to truth, which, we now understand, is the ascetic ideal in its purest form. This means, of course, that the atheism he celebrates in this section is neither 'unconditional' nor 'honest', for it has failed thus far to acknowledge its underlying faith in truth as a condition of its progress and success. These atheists may have forbidden themselves 'the *lie involved in belief in God*', but they have not yet forbidden themselves the lie involved in stipulating the inestimable value of truth. Here we should note that Nietzsche explicitly includes himself in this group of atheists, which is as close as he comes in GM to placing himself and his 'we' among the 'last idealists' described in Section 24.

He then refers his readers to GS 357, where we find his answer to the question: '*What*, in all strictness, has really *conquered* the Christian God?' The passage imported from GS 357 begins by describing the self-conquest of Christianity (which he later identifies as an instance of the 'self-cancellation' that 'all great things' are obliged by law to undergo) and it ends with a discussion of the 'self-overcoming' to which he and his friends are the rightful 'heirs'.[119] These two processes are joined by the scientific 'rigour' that he and his fellow 'good Europeans' practise as a matter of their refined 'conscience',[120] which demands of them 'intellectual cleanliness at any price'.

By appealing at this particular point in his narrative to the passage imported from GS 357, Nietzsche means to impress upon his best readers that he and they occupy a node of historical transformation, wherein the simple act of truth-telling might catalyse the self-conquest of Christianity. If *they* were to tell the truth about truth itself, he thus implies, the demise of Christian morality would be sealed. Immediately following the imported passage, he invokes the heretofore unknown 'law of life', which commands submission in all things, great and small:

> All great things bring about their own destruction through an act of self-cancellation: thus the law of life will have it, the law of the necessity of 'self-overcoming' in the nature of life – the lawgiver himself eventually receives the call: '*patere legem, quam ipse tulisti.*'

This appeal to the 'law of life' is apparently meant to announce the imminent convergence of the two processes described in the imported passage. Nietzsche thus presents his readers with the tantalizing possibility that their seemingly unremarkable labours of *self-overcoming* may converge with, and actually facilitate, the *self-cancellation* of Christian morality.

Maintaining the indirect mode of communication that he employs throughout Sections 23–27, Nietzsche does not identify the lawgivers who are called – in Latin, no less! – to submit to their own legislations. From what he has said thus far, however, we may assume that he means himself and his best readers, those 'unconditional honest atheists' whom the imported passage identifies as 'good Europeans'. Having boldly ruled against the Christian God, they are now called to rule against the god that resides within them. As the imported passage indicates, moreover, they are uniquely qualified, by virtue of the 'rigour' with which their conscience asserts itself, to submit to their own legislations. Having called to order the entirety of European civilization, they now must call themselves to order. Finally demanding of themselves the 'intellectual cleanliness' that they have required of others, they must turn their conscience against its vital, sustaining core: the will to truth. They must no longer rely on an unconfirmed faith in the saving power of truth.

He continues: Christian truthfulness, which is all that remains viable in Christian morality, will draw its *'most striking inference'*, – i.e. 'its inference against itself' – 'when it poses the question *"what is the meaning of all will to truth?"*' Although Nietzsche does not name the agent(s) who will pose this question on behalf of Christian truthfulness, the question itself calls to mind the 'task' he earlier defined for himself and his readers (GM III: 24). We are thus meant to conclude, apparently, that *they* will represent Christian truthfulness in its finest hour, as it issues a mortal challenge to Christian morality.[121] By steering the will to truth into an unprecedented confrontation with itself, that is, they will reveal that it rests on an unacknowledged *faith* in truth, about which it has been anything but truthful. As we have seen, moreover, their challenge to morality ultimately must be *self*-critical,[122] for *they* are the last true disciples of the morality they now seek to destroy. The will to truth will finally become 'conscious of itself as a *problem*', that is, in and through the experiments that he and his friends perform on themselves.

Here we gain our clearest sense of what is involved in the *wisdom* that Nietzsche has trained his warriors to attract (GM III: E).[123] As decreed by the 'law of life', the lawgiver is obliged to submit to his own legislations. As we have seen, however, the lawgiver also receives the *call* to submit, which, presumably, he may either heed or ignore. Although he is obliged to submit in any event, his receptivity to this call allows him to do so as an expression of his own will. The proof of wisdom thus lies in affirming the necessity of one's own self-overcoming, which one may accomplish by aligning one's will with the 'law of life'. 'Wisdom always loves only a warrior' (GM III: I), that is, because warriors cultivate virtues that are conducive to a heightened state of receptivity. Warriors are *unconcerned* with respect to themselves and their claims on life; they are *mocking* with respect to everything (including morality and truth) that humankind takes seriously; and they are *violent* with respect to everything that offers them worthy resistance in their pursuit of ever greater expenditures of strength (GM III: E). If Nietzsche's readers are wise, they will receive *and* heed the call to submit voluntarily to the laws they have prescribed to others. If his readers are not yet wise, they will either ignore the call or assume it to be addressed to other lawgivers. In that event, they will experience their inevitable submission to the 'law of life' as contrary to their will and, perhaps, as an objection to life itself.

This section ends with some fairly large promises, which, following Nietzsche's lead in Essay II, we should examine for their permissibility. In issuing these promises, he neither cuts himself off nor defers to someone 'younger, "heavier with future," and stronger' (GM II: 25), as he did at the close of Essay II. Perhaps we are meant to understand that *he* has grown 'younger, "heavier with future," and stronger' as a result of the war he has waged on the ascetic ideal.[124] With a clear (and 'intellectually clean') conscience, presumably, he confidently promises that

> As the will to truth thus gains self-consciousness – there can be no doubt of that – morality will gradually *perish* now. This is the great spectacle in a hundred acts reserved for the next two centuries in Europe – the most terrible, most questionable, and perhaps also the most hopeful of all spectacles.[125]

If there is 'no doubt' that the will to truth will become conscious of itself as a problem, and that Christian morality will perish as a result, then Nietzsche and his unknown friends need do nothing to bring these events to pass. The important question thus becomes whether, and how, they will involve themselves in the spectacle that is about to unfold. Will the collapse of Christian morality simply happen to them, or will they actively promote it? Will they experience themselves as helpless victims of this calamity, or as its proud, triumphant hosts? Will they endure this spectacle as passive spectators, or will they take the stage as players in their own right?

The stakes of their participation are by no means trivial. If they are successful in hosting the final act in the self-overcoming of morality, the will to truth shall draw its final, fatal inference *in and through them*. In that event, they will be divested, and perhaps violently so, of their faith in truth, their reliance on the ascetic ideal, and their residual allegiance to Christian morality. As the image of metamorphosis is meant to convey (GM III: 10), the host of a transformation of this magnitude – whether caterpillar or ascetic priest – is not likely to survive its defining display of hospitality. Were Nietzsche and his unknown friends to survive this assault on Christian morality – and their survival is by no means assured in GM – they might find themselves gasping in vain for the rarefied 'air' of their 'unconditional honest atheism'. As we shall see more clearly in the next section, in fact, the task for which Nietzsche recruits these unknown friends might be fairly described as a *suicide mission*.[126]

He closes this section on a note that is equally gloomy and hopeful. The centuries to come, he promises, will witness cataclysms and convulsions that may excite our desire for self-annihilation and consign the human species to extinction. Alternately, these very same disruptions may contribute to the self-overcoming of morality, the installation of a post-ascetic ideal, and the dawning of an extra-moral epoch in human history. As we have seen, everything rests on how Nietzsche's readers respond to the spectacle that is about to unfold. If they have not succeeded in making themselves worthy of wisdom, they are likely to receive the collapse of Christian morality as a devastating blow to their efforts to lead a meaningful existence. If they are wise, however, they will take their place onstage, positioning themselves to behold – and affirm – the extra-moral future that lies ahead.

Section 28

Here Nietzsche reviews his main narrative, especially as it has been advanced over the course of Essay III. He is particularly concerned, finally, to conclude his alternative account of the meaning of ascetic ideals.

He begins by adding a crucial element to his explanation of the 'most fundamental change' that occurred in the developmental history of the human animal (GM II: 16). Here, in the final section of GM, he finally explains what happened to the *will* when it was suddenly disengaged from the closed system of instinctual regulation in which it had previously operated:

> *This* is precisely what the ascetic ideal means: that something was *lacking*, that the human being was surrounded by a fearful *void* – he did not know how to justify, to account for, to affirm himself . . . There was no answer to the crying question, '*why* do I suffer?'

This unnamed 'something', the absence of which engendered a 'fearful void', was identified in the aphorism that Nietzsche prefixed to Essay III. There he explained that the 'basic fact of the human will . . . [is] its *horror vacui*: it *needs* a goal – and it will rather will *nothingness* than *not* will' (GM III: 1).

Prior to the unprecedented change described in GM II: 16, the human animal naturally pursued the goal that it shared with all animals – namely, the attainment of 'an optimum of favourable conditions under which it can expend all its strength and achieve its maximal feeling of power' (GM III: 7). Suddenly prevented from relying on its instincts, and newly burdened with the self-inflicted suffering that afflicts all parties to civil society, the human animal was no longer able to conduct business as usual. It was obliged for the first time to determine for itself a goal, the pursuit of which would deliver the feeling of power to which it had grown accustomed. Nietzsche thus treats the option of *not willing* – i.e. of failing (or refusing) to achieve the threshold level of affective investment that produces the desired feeling of power – as simply not viable. In order to live, to thrive and to grow, the human animal is obliged to *will* – i.e. to sustain its affective engagement with the world – even if it has no choice but to will the destruction of the conditions of its own existence.

For a time, however, no such goal presented itself. Unable to project its will into a suddenly insecure future, the human animal was compelled to ask after the very meaning of its painfully aimless existence. An existential crisis ensued, and the prospect of 'suicidal nihilism' became both likely and desirable. In response to this crisis, life devised the ascetic ideal, which, through the ministry of the ascetic priest, persuaded these sickly animals to continue to live, despite – or, more precisely, on account of – their existential suffering. The ascetic ideal deflated their crisis by providing them with a meaningful interpretation of their suffering: they suffered because they *deserved* to suffer. On the advice of the priest, that is, the human animal contracted the species-preserving illness of the bad conscience.

Nietzsche goes on to reveal the psychological principle that explains the seemingly irresistible attraction of the ascetic ideal. Contrary to popular opinion, human beings do '*not* repudiate suffering as such', but desire it and 'even seek it out', provided they are 'shown a *meaning* for it'. As we have seen, the ascetic ideal not only enabled these miserable, caged animals to interpret their suffering, but also trained them to crave the suffering – and attendant anaesthesia – that is reserved for guilty sinners. By burdening the human animal with a goal that it could neither attain nor disavow, the ascetic ideal saved the will. Nietzsche is quick to add, however, that the ascetic ideal owes its enormous influence not to any positive attributes of its own, but to the monopoly it has enjoyed in the business of conferring meaning. This is a significant addition to his earlier account of the ascetic ideal, for it explains, finally, why such a destructive ideal was able to amass such monstrous power:

> not, as people may believe, because God is at work behind the priests, but *faute de mieux* – because it was the only ideal so far, because it had no rival. (EH: gm)

Hence Nietzsche's answer to the guiding question of Essay III: the preponderance of ascetic ideals *means* that no other ideal has presented itself for consideration and adoption.[127] Throughout the entirety of the moral period of human history, under the civilizing regime of culture, human beings have had no choice but to embrace the ascetic ideal. Humankind is ascetic, that is, neither by nature nor by choice, but simply owing to the dearth of alternative ideals available to it. For reasons as yet unknown to us, life has required all human beings to pursue their projects of self-improvement and self-perfection under the banner of the ascetic ideal. Now that the moral stage in the development of the human animal is nearing its end, Nietzsche anticipates the rise of another ideal, around which the successor epoch might organize its defining activities.[128] In the successor epoch, he hopes, the pursuit of other, extra-ascetic goals will provide human beings with the feeling of vitality and purpose that will enable their continued survival.

A final layer of meaning remains to be exposed. Shifting abruptly to the present tense, Nietzsche issues his best readers one final challenge:

> We can no longer conceal from ourselves *what* is expressed by all that willing which has taken its direction from the ascetic ideal . . . all this means – let us dare to grasp it – *a will to nothingness* . . .

This is the point toward which Essay III has been steadily, if erratically, building.[129] What the preponderance of ascetic ideals *means*, in the end, is that the survival thus far of the human animal has been secured on the strength of a veiled expression of the *will to nothingness*. The ascetic ideal has enabled the human animal to attain a sustaining sense of meaning and purpose, but only on the condition of its unsuspecting participation in a campaign to destroy the very conditions of its existence. Nietzsche fears, that is, that nature's success in breeding a responsible animal has been achieved at the expense of the future of humankind. Although nature has thus far selected the human animal for survival, it has done so in a way that diminishes the likelihood of future selections.

Until very recently, the ascetic ideal has succeeded in closing the door to suicidal nihilism. It has done so, we now realize, by promoting a goal – namely, self-deprivation – whose pursuit enrols its adherents in a cleverly disguised programme of protracted self-annihilation. Rather than banish the will to nothingness, the ascetic ideal has simply (and artfully) disguised it 'under the cover of holy intentions' (GM III: 21). The promise of salvation has provided ascetics of all stripes with a useful pretext for distinguishing in all sincerity between their honourable practice of self-deprivation and the dishonourable practice of suicide. According to Nietzsche, however, this ingenious ruse has very nearly exhausted its usefulness to the species. As the authority of the ascetic ideal has declined, its clientele has steadily dwindled. Over most human beings, in fact, the ascetic ideal no longer wields any meaningful influence. As a deterrent to 'suicidal nihilism', which is the purpose for which it arose, it is no longer generally effective.

In some human beings, however, the ascetic ideal remains an effective impetus toward self-improvement and self-perfection. As we have seen, Nietzsche appeals to the ascetic ideal as he exhorts the 'last idealists' among his readers to host a final, fatal act of self-examination on the part of the will to truth. Inasmuch as their will to truth 'take[s] its direction from the ascetic ideal', however, it too must shelter a will to nothingness. This means that Nietzsche and his unknown friends, *qua* champions of the ascetic ideal, share a common will to destroy the last remaining conditions of their own existence. For example, although they are reliant on the will to truth for their identity and sense of purpose, they nevertheless find the 'meaning' of their 'whole being' in their campaign to compel the will to truth to become 'conscious of itself as a *problem*' (GM III: 27). Here it finally becomes clear that Nietzsche intends to harness the destructive power of the will to nothingness for his assault on the collapsing framework of Christian morality. In offering to host the demise of Christian morality, he and his unknown friends would effectively declare war on the very conditions under which they have managed to secure for themselves a meaningful existence.

Nietzsche's share in the will to nothingness thus explains his occasional expression of the wish – unmistakably, a martyr's wish – to be consumed in the process of engineering the collapse of Christian morality.[130] Those readers who agree to join him in this task will do so, presumably, on the strength of their wish to experience the quasi-erotic joy that he associates with acts of gratuitous, self-consuming destruction. In this respect, it may be to Nietzsche's credit that he offers his readers no real assurances that they will survive this assault on the stubborn remains of Christian morality. The objective of their mission is to host the self-destruction of morality, even at their own expense,[131] so that humankind might continue to undergo the transformations that will best ensure its selection for survival.

This is the essence of the wisdom that Nietzsche wishes to impart to the target audience of GM, which is why he begins Essay III by enlisting Zarathustra to exhort his readers to become warriors. Only as warriors can they can gain the wisdom that is expressed in an 'unconcerned', indifferent attachment to one's own existence (GM III: E).[132] Indeed, we are finally in a position to see that Nietzsche and his unknown friends will distinguish themselves from the ascetic priest only by virtue of the manner of their death. Whereas the priest simply refuses the call to submit, clinging tenaciously to the last degenerating form of life, Nietzsche and his friends take the physician's oath to heart,[133] timing their own self-destruction so that it also destroys all other instances of advanced degeneration. In doing so, they will arrange for themselves what Nietzsche elsewhere calls a *'natural* death', which is distinguished from its unnatural counter-part by virtue of being freely and consciously chosen by those who resolve to die 'without accident, without ambush' (TI 9: 36).

What does the decline of the ascetic ideal mean for those of us who do not join Nietzsche in his self-consuming assault on Christian morality? According to his diagnosis of our current predicament, most of us are already accustomed to living without an orienting ideal. While some of us are tempted by the prospect of suicidal nihilism, most of us manage to derive an adequate sense of meaning and purpose from the various tasks and routines that shape our lives. These tasks and routines may not be the stuff of legend, but they manage to keep us busy, productive, functional and reasonably content. (In this respect, we may resemble the 'last man' more closely than we care to admit [Z P5].[134]) To be sure, our sense of content-ment may be both artificial and fleeting, especially if it rests on our residual faith in the dead God. When the full meaning of the death of God finally overtakes us, we may discover that we cannot live without the direction and purpose that an orienting ideal provides.

Still, Nietzsche remains hopeful that humankind may survive the decline of the ascetic ideal. Over the course of its long reign, and especially over the past two millennia, the ascetic ideal has changed us, remade us in its image, and bred in us what has become our native artistry. It has made us moral, which is an unavoidable, if regrettable, precondition of becoming extra-moral. It has habituated us to the various self-regarding relationships in which we now stand, and it has accustomed us to the self-inflicted suffering and delayed gratification that these relationships entail. It has endowed us with spirit, occasionally in excess capacities, which the new philosopher may help us to put to some future, albeit as-yet-unspecified, use. Most importantly for Nietzsche's purposes in GM, the reign of the ascetic ideal has positioned humankind to complete the 'breeding' project that nature has established (and subsequently revised) for us. However unlikely this completion may seem, especially in light of the calamities and upheavals that await us, it remains possible *only* as a result of the formative influence of the ascetic ideal.

Summary

Essay III of GM reveals that ascetic ideals have meant many things to various constituencies, including *artists, philosophers, priests, scholars* and *warriors*. This diversity of meanings in turn means that the preponderance of ascetic ideals is endemic to the civilizing regime of culture, which has enabled the human animal to survive its involuntary estrangement from its natural instincts. The ascetic ideal has held sway, that is, not because human beings are ascetic by nature, but because no alternative ideal has presented itself for adoption.

As this period draws to a close, however, it has become clear that the ascetic ideal is in decline. Now that the death of God is ever more widely acknowledged, the ascetic ideal is no longer able to issue a generally credible promise of salvation through suffering. As the authority of the ascetic ideal continues to fade, moreover, we are finally able to discern the secret of its success: the ascetic ideal has saved the human animal by exciting the will to nothingness. Under the aegis of the ascetic ideal, the human animal sustains its baseline feeling of power and vitality, but only by virtue of its unsuspecting efforts to destroy the conditions of its very existence. In securing the immediate future of the human animal, that is, the ascetic ideal has placed the long-term future of the species in doubt. Fearing that any further reliance on the ascetic ideal may consign the human species to extinction, Nietzsche endeavours to accelerate the decline of the ascetic ideal and the concomitant collapse of Christian morality.

Hoping to capitalize on the unique opportunity afforded him by his historical situation, Nietzsche invites his best readers, whom he indirectly identifies as the last champions of the ascetic ideal, to join him in hosting the final act in the self-destruction of Christian morality. Acting as agents of Christian truthfulness, they will experimentally call into question the value of truth, intending thereby to compel the will to truth to acknowledge its reliance on a *faith* in truth. Their success in this venture would signal the death of Christian morality and the birth of a new, extra-moral epoch. Of course, Nietzsche and his unknown friends are likely to perish in the process, which is why he has recommended their training in the particular martial virtues cited by Zarathustra in the Epigraph to Essay III. Presumably, the unknown friends who join him in this final assault on Christian morality will share his wish to be consumed in the process of liberating humankind from the ascetic ideal.

Study questions
1. What is the *ascetic ideal*, and what is its primary function?
2. What is the significance of the 'maternal' philosopher, as described by Nietzsche?
3. Who is the *ascetic priest*, and what was his role in the 'slave revolt in morality'?
4. Why does Nietzsche insist that the ascetic priest is *not* a genuine physician?
5. What is the *will to nothingness*, and how might we prepare for its arrival?

CHAPTER 4

RECEPTION AND INFLUENCE

INITIAL RECEPTION AND INFLUENCE

The publication of GM in 1887 coincided with a general increase of interest throughout Europe in Nietzsche and his writings. Although he continued to lament the quantity and quality of his readers, he was very much aware of his arrival on the European intellectual scene. In the very next year, conscious of the expanding sphere of his influence, he would write:

> [E]verywhere else [excepting Germany] I have readers – nothing but first-rate intellects and proven characters, trained in high positions and duties. I even have real geniuses among my readers. In Vienna, in St Petersburg, in Stockholm, in Copenhagen, in Paris, in New York – (EH: 'good books' 2)

His reference to Copenhagen is particularly noteworthy, for it pertains directly to the initial reception and influence of GM. Upon receiving a complimentary copy of GM, the well-known Danish author Georg Brandes (1842–1927) replied to Nietzsche by writing, 'You are one of the few men with whom I should like to speak.'[1] Flattered by this invitation, Nietzsche responded with a gregarious letter of his own, and the two men began to correspond. Deeming his new acquaintances 'without doubt the most exciting of all German writers',[2] Brandes prepared a series of public lectures on Nietzsche, which he presented in the Spring of 1888 at the University of Copenhagen.[3] Drawing extensively on his reading of GM, Brandes characterized Nietzsche's philosophy as comprising an 'aristocratic radicalism',[4] which Nietzsche in turn judged to be 'the cleverest thing' he had ever read about himself.[5] (In a subsequent letter to another correspondent, Nietzsche proudly drew attention to the 'wondrous and almost mysterious respect' accorded him by 'all radical parties (Socialists, Nihilists, anti-Semites, Orthodox Christians, Wagnerians)'.[6]) Ten years later, Brandes had occasion to reflect on just how influential Nietzsche had become, remarking that Nietzsche's 'name has since flown round the world and is at this moment one of the most famous among our contemporaries'.[7] Of course, the extent of his fame remained utterly unknown to Nietzsche, who was stricken by madness in 1889. His final note to Brandes, postmarked 4 January 1889, was signed *The Crucified*.[8]

As this anecdote suggests, the publication of GM contributed to a general explosion of interest in Nietzsche's writings. Throughout Europe in the 1890s, Nietzsche was acclaimed as a leading thinker of the age, despite, as Brandes noted, his opposition to all of the 'instincts' that defined *fin de siècle* European culture.[9] In fact, the early reception of GM was remarkably diverse. Nietzsche's inspiration was claimed by representatives of parties and movements ranging across and beyond the political spectrum. Whereas Brandes praised Nietzsche for his untimely aristocratic sympathies, other critics denounced his writings as conducive to the spread of a general perception of dislocation and chaos at the end of the century. For example, the influential psychologist Max Nordau (1849–1923) decried Nietzsche's unhealthy influence on would-be anarchists, individualists and freedom-seekers.[10] 'Without doubt,' Nordau observed in 1892, 'the real Nietzsche gang consists of born imbecile criminals, and of simpletons drunk with sonorous words.'[11] In an effort to corroborate his diagnosis of Nietzsche's besetting 'ego-mania', Nordau cited liberally from GM, whose central claims, he insisted, could be traced to their 'source' in the author's overpowering 'Sadism'.[12]

As the severity of this judgement confirms the early reception of GM was not entirely to Nietzsche's credit. While responses like Nordau's were easily countered, other, darker readings of GM proved to be more serious and persistent. Notwithstanding his ridicule of the so-called 'master race' (GM I: 5), his praise for the 'popular-moral genius' of the Jews (GM I: 16), his mockery of Wagner's *Parsifal* (GM III: 3–4), his dismissive treatment of Luther (GM III: 22), his express contempt for anti-Semites and Aryan enthusiasts (GM III: 27), and his diagnosis of 'the undeniable and palpable stagnation of the German spirit' (GM III: 27), he was received by many readers as a thinker sympathetic to the xenophobic nationalism that was on the rise in Bismarck's Germany. Later, in the twentieth century, the polemical style and inflammatory rhetoric of GM attracted a devoted readership among anti-Semites and German nationalists,[13] including the Nazi ideologue Alfred Bäumler.[14]

As many scholars have observed, the appropriation of Nietzsche by anti-Semites, German nationalists, Aryan supremacists and Nazi apologists was possible only on the basis of an extremely selective reading, if not an aggressive misreading, of his actual writings. Of course, precisely this kind of misreading was encouraged by his sister, Elisabeth Förster-Nietzsche, who, upon returning to Germany from her failed adventure in colonial Paraguay, schemed to present her brother as a kind of all-purpose prophet of right-wing extremism.[15] Her legion of allies and flatterers included Mussolini and Hitler, both of whom, she was convinced, embodied the spirit of her brother's philosophy.

Notwithstanding the opportunistic machinations of his sister, we should beware of concluding that the particular misreading that eventually informed the Nazi appropriation of Nietzsche was conjured from thin air. Although Nietzsche was in no sense a proto-Nazi, he is certainly responsible for the provocative, 'polemical' aims of GM, as well as for the rhetorical countermeasures deployed in their service. In particular, as we have seen, he is responsible for electing a high-stakes rhetorical strategy that encouraged his readers to project their anti-Semitic prejudices onto him. Well aware that his *Zarathustra* had attracted the interest of excitable anti-Semites, he might have reconsidered some of the more readily – and more predictably – misunderstood references and allusions in GM.

He also bears some measure of responsibility for failing to discourage more vigorously and categorically the misinterpretations of GM that were bound to proliferate. For example, his express wish to discourage his admirers among the anti-Semites is not easily squared with his recourse in GM to some fairly standard negative stereotypes of Jews. Having proposed 'Rome against Judea, Judea against Rome' as a 'symbol' for the struggle that has defined European history and culture (GM I: 16), he surely knew (or should have suspected) that some of his readers would be keen to adopt GM for their pro-imperial and anti-Semitic causes. Similarly, his reluctance to name Christianity and St Paul as the primary targets of his critique in GM – a rhetorical ploy he abandoned when writing *The Antichrist* and his review of GM in *Ecce Homo* – should have led him to suspect that some readers would mistake GM for a pro-Christian screed. Of course, Nietzsche is also famous for claiming not to care what use his merely modern readers make of him. If we take this claim seriously as a genuine expression of his authentic wishes – which I do not recommend – then it might be said of Nietzsche and GM have attracted precisely the readership that they deserve.

LATER INFLUENCES OF GM

Nietzsche's appeal in GM to the unconscious, amoral drives that motivate human behaviour exerted a profound influence on the development of both depth psychology and psychoanalysis. Particularly noteworthy in this respect is his influence on the pioneering figures in these fields of research, including Sigmund Freud (1856–1939), Carl Jung (1875–1961) and Alfred Adler (1870–1937).

The central hypothesis of Essay II, pertaining to the introjection of animal aggression that is required of all civilized human beings (GM II: 16), has been particularly influential. This hypothesis was taken up and developed by no less an authority than Freud, who installed a similar account of the origins of civilization at the centre of his 1929 masterpiece, *Civilization and Its Discontents*.[16] Linking the achievement of happiness to the spontaneous gratification of the instincts, Freud confirmed Nietzsche's suspicion that the escalating demands of self-surveillance, self-deprivation and self-castigation are sufficiently onerous as to ensure the unhappiness (or 'discontent') of civilized human beings.[17] If we are to enjoy the relative peace and prosperity of civil society, he surmised, we must develop strategies for coping with the non-negotiable discontents that attend the inward discharge of our aggressive, destructive energies. The future of humankind, Freud concluded, may belong either to Eros or to death.[18]

The influence of GM was propagated through Freud to a number of scholars who were similarly concerned to explore the broader sociological implications of Nietzsche's hypothesis. In *Eros and Civilization* (1966), Herbert Marcuse (1898–1979) appealed to Nietzsche to correct for what he regarded as Freud's overly pessimistic view of civilization. Echoing the potentially hopeful note on which Nietzsche concludes GM, Marcuse raised the possibility of a less exacting version of the Reality Principle, which might prove friendlier to spontaneous expressions of Eros. The influence of GM, and especially its controversial diagnosis of the sickliness of contemporary society, is also discernible in the work of other social psychologists, including Eric Fromm (1900–80), Rollo May (1904–94) and Norman O. Brown (1913–2002).

The larger sociological implications of Nietzsche's diagnosis of late modern European culture influenced a number of prominent writers of the twentieth century. Authors as diverse as G. B. Shaw (1856–1950), D. H. Lawrence (1885–1930), Hermann Hesse (1877–1962), Thomas Mann (1875–1955), André Gide (1869–1951), Franz Kafka (1883–1924) and Nikos Kazantzakis (1883–1957) were inspired by Nietzsche to analyse the discontents of the modern world – including repression, guilt, despair, alienation and anxiety – and to explore the possibility that certain individuals might succeed in escaping (or postponing) the stifling demands of civilization. More generally, Nietzsche is recognized as one of the progenitors of the *existentialist* movement in philosophy and literature, which it was concerned to muster an affirmative, authentic response to the crisis attending the 'death of God'. His influence on the development of existentialism is most obviously evident in the writings of Martin Heidegger (1889–1976), John-Paul Sartre (1905–80), Albert Camus (1913–60), Martin Buber (1878–1965), Paul Tillich (1886–1965) and Andre Malraux (1901–76).

Nietzsche is also widely recognized for his contributions to the 'hermeneutics of suspicion' that spurred the development of literary, aesthetic, political and cultural criticism in the twentieth century. According to the philosopher Paul Ricoeur (1913–2005), Nietzsche should be regarded as a 'master of suspicion',[19] who, along with Marx and Freud,

> clear[ed] the horizon for a more authentic word, for a new reign of Truth, not only by means of a 'destructive' critique, but by the invention of an art of *interpreting*.[20]

The unique 'art of interpreting' developed by Nietzsche inspired twentieth-century readers to challenge orthodoxies across a wide range of human endeavours, including philosophy, science, history, literature, religion, art, psychoanalysis and politics. As we see in

GM, for example, Nietzsche employs his novel 'art of interpreting' to expose hoary moral prejudices, to overturn established conventions, to subvert received wisdom and to bathe the bloated idols of late modern European culture in the unflattering light of genealogical criticism. As we also see in GM, he raises these suspicions not simply to entertain his readers, but also to acquaint them with the prejudices that they are least inclined on their own to question and confront. A regimen of elevated suspicion is needed, he believes, because we 'moderns' have become complicit in our own diminution and destruction. Through the practice of morality, our highest hopes and aspirations for ourselves have become dangerously entangled with the will to nothingness.

The new 'art of interpreting' displayed in GM also influenced some of the leading figures associated with the development of critical theory, including the Frankfurt School stalwarts Theodor Adorno (1903–63) and Max Horkheimer (1895–1973). Their collaborative work, *Dialectic of Enlightenment* (1947), developed some of the insights displayed in Nietzsche's critique of science in Essay III of GM. His influence as a 'master of suspicion' is also evident in the writings of twentieth-century philosophers and critics such as Paul de Man (1919–83), Jacques Derrida (1930–2004), Maurice Blanchot (1907–2003), Sarah Kofman (1934–94) and Gilles Deleuze (1925–95). In their own diverse ways, these writers attempt, first of all, to cultivate Nietzsche's genealogical practice of questioning the unquestionable; and second, to apply this practice to specific textual, social, legal and political concerns.

The influence of GM on research in the social sciences is most evident in the development of post-structuralist approaches to history and anthropology. One of Nietzsche's most prominent heirs was the French historian and philosopher Michel Foucault (1926–84), who, openly acknowledging his debt to Nietzsche, occasionally conducted his own research under the rubric of 'genealogy'. Much as Nietzsche endeavoured in GM to acquaint the most dutiful practitioners of science with their unacknowledged faith in truth, so Foucault sought to expose the prejudices and power relations that silently inform the governing discourses of the social sciences. In *The Order of Things* (1966) Foucault undertakes an 'archaeology' of the social sciences, which enables him to chart the epistemic convergence that made the practice of modern science possible. In *Discipline and Punish: The Birth of the Prison* (1975), he builds on, and develops, the seminal discussion of punishment found in Essay II of GM. Finally, his three-volume investigation into *The History of Sexuality* offers a genealogy of the modern subject, especially as this subject came to be defined in the context of 'scientific' attempts to define sexual normalcy and deviancy.

The influence of GM on the development of anthropology and ethnology is confirmed by Gilles Deleuze and Félix Guattari, who declare in their *Anti-Oedipus* (1972) that GM should be considered 'the great book of modern ethnology'.[21] They are especially impressed by the emphasis placed in GM on the need for primitive human societies to *create* the conditions of human collectivity, through the memory-inducing processes of 'inscribing', 'coding' and 'marking' the body.[22]

CHAPTER 5

NOTES FOR FURTHER READING

Readers who wish to continue their study of Nietzsche may sample from a wealth of valuable commentaries in the Anglophone secondary literature. Walter Kaufmann's groundbreaking book, *Nietzsche: Philosopher, Psychologist, Antichrist* (Princeton University Press, 1950), remains an accessible, informed guide to the major themes of Nietzsche's philosophy. Kaufmann's book is especially notable for its attention to the internal coherence of Nietzsche's seemingly disparate teachings and insights.

More recent interpretations of note include: Richard Schacht's *Nietzsche* (Routledge & Kegan Paul, 1983), which offers an exhaustive survey of Nietzsche's contributions to traditional philosophical debates; Alexander Nehamas's *Nietzsche: Life as Literature* (Harvard University Press, 1985), which examines Nietzsche's philosophy in terms of his attempt to present his own life on the model of a well-drawn literary character; Alan White's *Within Nietzsche's Labyrinth* (Routledge, 1990), which endeavours to penetrate to the affirmative core of Nietzsche's darkest teachings; Paul van Tongeren's *Reinterpreting Modern Culture* (Purdue University Press, 2000), which provides a comprehensive introduction to Nietzsche's critical engagements with contemporary culture; David Allison's *Reading the New Nietzsche* (Rowman & Littlefield, 2000), which offers lively, readable interpretations of four of Nietzsche's most important books (including GM); and Robert Solomon's *Living with Nietzsche* (Oxford University Press, 2003), which accounts for Nietzsche's enduring appeal as an existential philosopher. In *The Good European: Nietzsche's Work Sites in Word and Image* (University of Chicago Press, 1997), David Krell and Donald Bates complement their instructive account of Nietzsche's philosophy with photographs of various settings in which Nietzsche lived and worked. Another valuable introduction to Nietzsche's philosophy can be found in the entry contributed by Robert Wicks to the *Stanford Encyclopedia of Philosophy* (at http://plato.stanford.edu/entries/ nietzsche/).

Excellent books of a more specialized focus include: John Wilcox's *Truth and Value in Nietzsche* (University of Michigan Press, 1974), which surveys Nietzsche's contributions to epistemology and value theory; Bernd Magnus' *Nietzsche's Existential Imperative* (Indiana University Press, 1978), which develops an influential interpretation of the doctrine of eternal recurrence; Gary Shapiro's *Nietzschean Narratives* (Indiana University Press, 1989), which untangles the narrative threads that inform Nietzsche's most ambitious works; Henry Staten's *Nietzsche's Voice* (Cornell University Press, 1990), which charts the 'libidinal economy' of Nietzsche's most personal writings; Maudemarie Clark's *Nietzsche on Truth and Philosophy* (Cambridge University Press, 1990), which conducts a careful analysis of Nietzsche's evolving understanding of the nature of truth; Alan Schrift's *Nietzsche and the Question of Interpretation* (Routledge, 1990), which measures Nietzsche's influence on the development of the hermeneutic tradition of European philosophy; Laurence Lampert's *Nietzsche and Modern Times* (Yale University Press, 1993), which situates Nietzsche, along with Bacon and Descartes, in the esoteric project of modern philosophy; Babette Babich's *Nietzsche's Philosophy of Science* (SUNY Press, 1994), which examines Nietzsche's critical engagement with the theory and practice of contemporary science; Graham Parkes's *Composing the Soul* (University of Chicago Press, 1994), which offers a comprehensive account of the development of Nietzsche's depth-psychological model; and R. Kevin Hill's *Nietzsche's Critiques* (Oxford University Press, 2003), which illuminates the Kantian structure of Nietzsche's critical method; Julian Young's *Nietzsche's Philosophy of Religion* (Cambridge University Press, 2006), which debunks Nietzsche's supposed atheism and isolates the core of his enduring religious commitments; and Bernard Reginster's *The Affirmation of Life* (Harvard University Press, 2006), which provides a careful assessment of Nietzsche's attempts to overcome nihilism. Edited volumes of note include *Nietzsche: A Critical Reader*, ed. Peter Sedgwick (Blackwell, 1995); *The Cambridge Companion to Nietzsche*, eds Bernd Magnus and Kathleen Higgins (Cambridge University Press, 1996); *Nietzsche*, eds John Richardson and Brian Leiter (Oxford University Press, 2001);

and *A Nietzschean Bestiary*, eds Ralph Acampora and Christa Davis Acampora (Rowman & Littlefield, 2004).

Several fine biographies of Nietzsche are available, including R. J. Hollingdale's *Nietzsche: The Man and his Philosophy* (Cambridge University Press, 2005); Ronald Hayman's *Nietzsche: A Critical Life* (Penguin, 1982); and Rüdiger Safranski's *Nietzsche: A Philosophical Biography* (W. W. Norton, 2002). Readers of GM may also be interested in two biographies of a more restricted focus: Ben MacIntyre's *Forgotten Fatherland* (Farrar Straus Giroux, 1992), which recounts the colonial and European misadventures of Elisabeth Förster-Nietzsche; and Robin Small's *Nietzsche and Rée: A Star Friendship* (Oxford University Press, 2005), which illuminates the formation and dissolution of Nietzsche's friendship with Dr Paul Rée.

Readers of GM who wish to gain a deeper understanding of *Thus Spoke Zarathustra* are in luck. Several valuable commentaries have been published in the past 25 years, including Laurence Lampert's *Nietzsche's Teaching* (Yale University Press, 1986); Kathleen Higgins' *Nietzsche's Zarathustra* (Temple University Press, 1987); Greg Whitlock's *Returning to Sils Maria* (Peter Lang, 1990); Stanley Rosen's *The Mask of Enlightenment* (Cambridge University Press, 1995); Robert Gooding-Williams' *Zarathustra's Dionysian Modernism* (Stanford University Press, 2001); and T. K. Seung's *Nietzsche's Epic of the Soul* (Lexington Books, 2005).

The past 30 years have also witnessed an explosion of interest in Nietzsche as a political thinker. Tracy Strong's landmark book, *Friedrich Nietzsche and the Politics of Transfiguration* (University of California Press, 1975), offers an extended treatment of Nietzsche's intended contributions to a radical refashioning of human beings and human society. In *Nietzsche and Political Thought* (MIT Press, 1988), Mark Warren examines Nietzsche's diagnosis of European nihilism and documents the limitations of his political thinking. Bruce Detwiler's *Nietzsche and the Politics of Aristocratic Radicalism* (University of Chicago Press, 1990) offers a sympathetic treatment of Nietzsche's experiment with radical politics. Leslie Paul Thiele's *Friedrich Nietzsche and the Politics of the Soul* (Princeton University Press, 1990) investigates the political implications of Nietzsche's preoccupation with the possibility of cultivating the soul of the heroic individual. In *An Introduction to Nietzsche as Political Thinker: The Perfect Nihilist* (Cambridge University Press, 1994),

NIETZSCHE'S *ON THE GENEALOGY OF MORALS*

Keith Ansell-Pearson judiciously weighs Nietzsche's various contributions to contemporary political philosophy. In *Nietzsche: The Ethics of an Immoralist* (Harvard University Press, 1995), Peter Berkowitz develops the intriguing thesis that Nietzsche's 'immoralism' actually points toward a goal – self-deification – that Nietzsche knew to be unattainable. David Owen's excellent study, *Nietzsche, Politics and Modernity* (Sage, 1995), offers a balanced assessment of Nietzsche's objections to the dominant political ideals of late modernity, particularly those associated with the rise of political liberalism. In *A Nietzschean Defense of Democracy* (Open Court, 1995), Lawrence Hatab mounts a spirited defence of an agonistic model of democracy that is meant to withstand Nietzsche's otherwise devastating repudiation of democratic movements and reforms. In *The Art of Power* (Lexington Books, 2007), Diego von Vacano examines the attempts by Nietzsche and Machiavelli to incorporate aesthetic form and content into political philosophy.

GM itself has been singled out for consideration by a number of talented scholars. Gilles Deleuze's breathtaking book, *Nietzsche and Philosophy* (Columbia University Press, 1983), contains an influential discussion of the 'movement' in Essay II from *ressentiment* to bad conscience. In *Anti-Oedipus*, (University of Minnesota Press, 1983), Deleuze and Félix Guattari rely extensively on GM as they develop a post-psychoanalytic critique of modern capitalism. Eric Blondel's learned book, *Nietzsche: The Body and Culture* (Stanford University Press, 1991), explores the continuities that inform the parallel projects involved in diagnosing bodies and cultures. In *Nietzsche's Genealogy* (Cornell University Press, 1995), Randall Havas deftly interprets GM (and other writings) as emblematic of Nietzsche's critical, historical method. Keith Ansell-Pearson's visionary book, *Viroid Life* (Routledge, 1997), translates the insights offered in GM into an articulation of the trans-human future that may follow in the wake of the 'death of God'. In *Nietzsche and the Problem of Sovereignty* (University of Illinois Press, 1997), Richard White develops an interpretation of GM (and other books) that illuminates the central concept of sovereignty (or mastery). Aaron Ridley's superb book, *Nietzsche's Conscience* (Cornell University Press, 1998), provides a sympathetic reconstruction of Nietzsche's main arguments in GM, while also exposing the lapses and tensions that trouble these arguments. Raymond Geuss's impressive collection of essays, *Morality, Culture, and*

History (Cambridge University Press, 1999), contains two chapters of direct relevance to the project of GM. In *Nietzsche's Ethics and his War on 'Morality'* (Oxford University Press, 1999), Simon May examines in depth the political context of Nietzsche's critical engagement with Christian morality. Brian Leiter's lapidary study, *Nietzsche on Morality* (Routledge, 2001), delivers a detailed commentary on some of the most important sections and arguments of GM. John Richardson's valuable book, *Nietzsche's New Darwinism* (Oxford University Press, 2004), provides a compelling interpretation of the version of natural selection that Nietzsche means to defend in GM (and elsewhere). David Owen's welcome new book, *Nietzsche's Genealogy of Morals* (Acumen, 2007), provides a rigorous, clear account of the intended contribution of GM to Nietzsche's 'revaluation of all values'. Finally, Christopher Janaway's recent study, *Beyond Selflessness: Reading Nietzsche's Genealogy* (Oxford University Press, 2007), offers a splendid close reading of GM, wherein the complexity of Nietzsche's struggle to distance himself from Schopenhauer and Rée is illuminated. Two edited volumes deserve mention here: Richard Schacht's *Nietzsche, Genealogy, Morality* (University of California Press, 1994); and Christa Davis Acampora's *Nietzsche's On the Genealogy of Morals: Critical Essays* (Rowman & Littlefield, 2006). Finally, the translations of GM that have been produced, respectively, by Clark and Swensen, Smith, and Diethe all appear in editions of GM that contain helpful introductory essays and explanatory notes.

NOTES

1. CONTEXT

1 Safranski, p. 316.
2 Hayman, p. 342.
3 Hayman, p. 311.
4 According to Kaufmann (p. 3), the title page of GM bears the following avowal: 'A Sequel to My Last Book, *Beyond Good and Evil*, Which It Is Meant to Supplement and Clarify.'
5 Thatcher, p. 588.
6 The German word is *Moral*, which Kaufmann and Hollingdale usually translate as *morality*, though in the title of GM, they prefer *morals*. This preference follows Kaufmann's practice in his translation of Nietzsche's title for Part Five of *Beyond Good and Evil*.
7 For more extended accounts of what Nietzsche meant by 'morality', see Leiter, pp. 78–81; and Owen, pp. 69–70.
8 He later suggests that GM is a response of sorts to Schopenhauer's *The World as Will and Representation*, which also 'was a "polemic" ' (GM P5).
9 After hearing from Georg Brandes that the 'Icelandic sagas' offer 'a great deal to confirm [his] hypotheses and theories concerning the morality of a master race' (Brandes, p. 87), Nietzsche related this compliment to his friend Heinrich Köselitz (Peter Gast) (SB 8, p. 324).
10 See Gemes, pp. 204–5; Leiter, pp. 180–1; and Janaway, pp. 249–52.

3. READING THE TEXT

1 Here I follow Clark and Swensen, who translate *wir Erkennenden* as 'we knowers' (p. 1).
2 Nietzsche and Rée spent the winter of 1876–7 together in Sorrento, at which time they discussed their similar ideas about the history of morality (Clark and Swensen, p. 122). Nietzsche refers to this winter in Section 2 of his Preface, but he does not mention Rée in this context.

3 'Our task,' he confirms elsewhere, is to '*question*' morality (GS 345).

4 See GS 382.

5 In this passage, Nietzsche also associates 'cheerfulness' with 'prankishness' [*Übermut*] (TI P).

6 See D P5.

7 Here I follow Ansell-Pearson, pp. 97–101.

8 I am indebted here to Clark, in Clark and Swensen (p. xxvi).

9 In a passage that was influential for this account of the priests, Nietzsche attributes the sickness of the priests to their internalization of the community's judgement of their deviations from the morality of mores (D 9).

10 See A 38.

11 A prominent theme of Nietzsche's 1888 writings is his identification of the priest as a *chandala* (or outcast), whom healthy societies and cultures should take pre-emptive measures to neutralize.

12 He later refers to this 'inversion' as involving a 'revaluation of all values' (GM I: 8).

13 He is far more explicit in his review of GM, where he explains, 'The truth of the first [Essay] is . . . the birth of Christianity out of the spirit of *ressentiment*' (EH: gm).

14 As Thatcher suggests (p. 589), *sub hoc signo* is probably meant to recall the motto of Constantine: *in hoc signo vinces*. See also Clark and Swensen, p. 135.

15 See Yovel, pp. 145–52.

16 As Yovel observes (pp. 149–50), the examples Nietzsche cites of Jewish hatred – e.g. the Apocalypse of John, the quartet of Jesus, Peter, Paul and Mary – are in fact more commonly understood as exemplary of early Christianity.

17 In providing this articulation, he relies heavily on the predecessor account – juxtaposing *master morality* and *slave morality* – found in BGE 260.

18 Here I prefer the translation suggested by Clark and Swensen (p. 19), which better conveys the organic connotation of the verb *herauswächsen*.

19 The designation 'men of *ressentiment*' refers more precisely to the slaves insofar as they have been transformed, and subsequently weaponized, by the priest. The designation may, but need not, include the priest himself.

20 Here it is interesting to note that one chapter of Nietzsche's autobiography is titled 'Why I Am So Clever'.

21 This may be a reference to the New Testament parable in which Jesus identifies 'the evil one' as the 'enemy' who has sown 'weeds' (= 'sons of the evil one') in the 'field' (= world) (Mt. 13.24–30, 36–9; cf. 1 Jn 5.19). Nietzsche also refers to this parable in the first speech of Part II of his *Zarathustra*.

22 He elsewhere confirms that the 'morality of *ressentiment* . . . is the Judaeo-Christian morality pure and simple' (A 24).

23 This division may be meant to reproduce the two phases of 'conceptual transformation' described in Section 5.

24 The men of *ressentiment*, whose enforced labor commanded the nobles, would have had no first-hand experience of the nobles as 'uncaged beasts of prey', who appear in 'wilderness' as 'triumphant monsters' (GM I: 11). They must have learned of these exploits from the priest, who *did* encounter these 'beasts of prey' in wilderness (GM III: 15).

25 A similar rhetorical construction elsewhere introduces his more explicit concern that 'it is indecent to be a Christian today. *And here begins my nausea*' (A 38).

26 What the respondent hears anticipates Nietzsche's later reference to this workshop, where he condemns its resident smiths for attempting 'to sanctify *revenge* under the name of *justice* . . . and to rehabilitate not only revenge but all *reactive* affects in general' (GM II: 11).

27 See A 45.

28 See BGE 260, on which this section is based.

29 See BGE 200.

30 See BGE 257, where Nietzsche describes the 'mysterious *pathos*' that bespeaks 'the craving for an ever new widening of distances within the soul itself . . .'

31 Yovel, p. 179.

32 'See with what large letters I am writing to you with my own hand' (Gal. 6.11).

33 See BGE 195, which Nietzsche recommended to his readers in Section 7. See also Yovel (p. 151); and Clark and Swensen (p. 138).

34 Following the suggestion of Clark and Swensen (p. 35), I have modified the Kaufmann and Hollingdale translation to reflect the 'permission' rather than the 'right' to 'make promises'. Diethe's suggestion of 'prerogative' (p. 35) is also preferable to 'right'. I am also indebted to Acampora, pp. 148–50.

35 I am indebted for this general line of interpretation to Richardson, especially pp. 11–15.

36 Acampora, pp. 148–50.

37 For further discussion of the morality of mores, see Clark and Swensen, pp. 140–1; and Leiter, pp. 226–9.

38 In one of the sections from *Dawn* that Nietzsche recommends here to the readers of GM, he explains that the morality of mores judged the 'free human being' to be 'immoral' (D 9).

39 'Supra-customary' would be a more literal, albeit less elegant, translation of *übersittliche* than 'supramoral'.

40 The recommended sections from *The Dawn* are particularly suggestive of a relationship between the sovereign individual and the *priestly* noble caste. For example, the list of priestly prescriptions offered in GM I: 6 bears a strong resemblance to the list provided in D 14. We may be meant to think of the knightly-aristocratic nobles as descended from a sovereign individual who is relatively untroubled by, and perhaps oblivious to, his offense against the customs and traditions of the collective; and of the priestly nobles as descended from a sovereign individual who internalizes the outrage of the offended collective.

41 For alternative interpretations of the sovereign individual, see Hatab, pp. 37–9; White, pp. 144–7; Acampora, pp. 146–56; Owen, pp. 96–107; and Janaway, pp. 116–20.

42 See Clark, in Clark and Swensen, p. xxvi.

43 See Clark, in Clark and Swensen, p. xxxi.

44 He will turn in the next section to the 'contractual relationship between *creditor* and *debtor*', and in Section 8 he will take up 'the fundamental forms of buying, selling, barter, trade, and traffic'.

45 Deleuze and Guattari, pp. 190–2.

46 See also BGE 260.

47 As we shall see, he may have in mind here those beasts of prey who founded the earliest 'state' (GM II: 17). In order to make use of their captives, these beasts of prey must have agreed at some point to temper and modulate their natural instinct for cruelty.

48 Here too I follow the suggestion of Clark and Swensen, p. 47.

49 I refer here to the 'handicap' theory advanced by Zahavi and Zahavi, especially in Chapters 2 and 12. I am indebted to Joseph Orkin (see Bibliography) both for this particular interpretation of the self-cancellation of justice for alerting me more generally to the important connections between Essay II of GM and the research conducted by the Zahavis.

50 While the 'institution of law' may be the 'most decisive' way to end 'the senseless raging of *ressentiment*', these well-intentioned noble individuals also, and disastrously, rely on religion – more precisely, on the intercession of the priest – to quell the *ressentiment* of the lower orders.

51 Here too I follow Richardson, pp. 20–6.

52 See TI 9: 14.

53 See BGE 13.

54 Spencer, pp. 444–5.

55 I am indebted here, and in general, to Ridley's treatment of conscience, pp. 15–22.

56 In his review of GM, Nietzsche treats this point as central to Essay II: 'The *second* inquiry [of GM] offers the psychology of the *conscience* – which is . . . the instinct of cruelty that turns back after it can no longer discharge itself externally' (EH: gm).

57 He earlier identified 'the man of *ressentiment*' as the one who 'has the invention of the "bad conscience" on his conscience' (GM II: 11).

58 A similar explanation is found at BGE 257.

59 While it may be the case that the illness of the bad conscience was first contracted by the victims of the predatory violence described in this section, the larger narrative of GM confirms that the agents of this violence eventually contracted this illness as well.

60 Here I follow Migotti, p. 114.

61 As Leiter observes (p. 236–7), the problem translators face here is that *Schuldgefühl* may be translated either as 'feeling of indebtedness' or 'feeling of guilt'. Diethe prefers the former translation (62), while Clark & Swensen opt for the latter (61–2). As we have seen, Kaufmann and Hollingdale first offer 'guilty feeling of indebtedness' and, later, 'feeling

of guilty indebtedness'. This particular problem is exacerbated by Nietzsche's concern in Essay II of GM to describe the transformation of the concept (and experience) of religious *debt* into the concept (and experience) of moral guilt. As a result, it is not entirely clear in this Section whether he wishes to refer to a 'feeling of indebtedness', a 'feeling of guilt', or some undefined feeling that combines elements of indebtedness and guilt. I prefer the Kaufmann and Hollingdale translation because it captures the indefinite, transitional status of the 'feeling' in question, especially as it may have been experienced by the early Christians whom Nietzsche discusses in this section. For an instructive discussions of this issue, see Risse, pp. 61–3; and Leiter, pp. 237–9.

62 Nietzsche believes that Paul popularized the notion that Jesus died not for the reasons enumerated by Pilate, but to atone for the sins of humankind (cf. 1 Cor. 15.3). See A 42, 45 and 48.

63 I have attempted in these paragraphs to combine an insight recorded by Risse (p. 65) with the interpretation advanced by Ridley (pp. 26–35).

64 See GM I: 13.

65 Ridley, pp. 32–3.

66 See EH: 'wise' 5.

67 See GS 382.

68 White, p. 146.

69 See GS 371, where Nietzsche implies that the one to whom he must defer is a later, changed version of *himself*.

70 My attention to the assertion in GM of Nietzsche's own conscience is indebted, of course, to Ridley. In light of Ridley's doubts about the role of 'exemplarity' in GM (pp. 154–5), however, he presumably would not endorse that particular element of my interpretation.

71 Here I follow the interpretation independently advanced by Wilcox, pp. 596–9, and by Janaway, pp. 169–70.

72 Nietzsche earlier employed a similar phrase – *Überzahl* (rather than *Mehrzahl*) *der Sterblichen* – to describe those who rely on 'the sublime self-deception that interprets weakness as freedom, and their being thus-and-thus as a *merit*' (GM I: 13).

73 I am indebted here to Clark, in Clark and Swensen, p. xxxiii. See Janaway, pp. 165–7.

74 See GS 358.

75 The 'case' of Wagner was sufficiently important to Nietzsche that in 1888 he devoted a short book to the topic.

76 See EH: hh 5.

77 See BGE 212.

78 Additional references to the possibility of a productive practice of asceticism are found at WP 915 and A 57.

79 See EH: 'clever' 39; GS 369; HH I P7.

80 He elsewhere describes his own self-misunderstanding as an expression of 'the supreme prudence' that governed his growth and development (EH: 'clever' 9).

81 Ridley draws a valuable distinction between ascetic *ideals* and ascetic *procedures* (p. 59).
82 See Ridley, pp. 66–7.
83 Here we may do well to recall that the 'sovereign individual', whom I have presented as a forebear of the noble priests and knights, similarly knew himself to arouse fear in others (GM II: 2).
84 Nietzsche may have in mind here the distinction between those who are mad (namely, the priests) and those who have no choice 'but to make themselves or pretend to be mad' (D 14).
85 This may be why Nietzsche cautions us not to 'think lightly' of the bad conscience simply on the basis of its 'initial painfulness and ugliness' (GM II: 18).
86 He confirms the truth of this supposition, at least with respect to himself, in EH: 'destiny' 4; and A 9, 13, 62.
87 Once again, I follow the translation suggested by Clark and Swensen (p. 85).
88 Having refrained in Section 6 from siding with either Kant or Stendhal, here he unambiguously rejects the position of the former and implicitly endorses the position of the latter.
89 For additional clarification, see Ridley pp. 108–15; Leiter, pp. 264–79; and Janaway, pp. 202–16.
90 Janaway, pp. 199–201.
91 I am indebted here to Janaway, pp. 193–201.
92 See TI 5: 1.
93 As Nietzsche explains elsewhere, his own mastery of multiple perspectives, as evidenced by his ability to 'reverse perspectives', has made him *wise* (EH: 'wise' 1), which, as the Epigraph to Essay III confirms, is what he also wishes for his readers.
94 Here I follow the suggestion of Clark and Swensen, p. 86.
95 Kaufmann and Hollingdale offer 'agent' here as their translation of the word – *Thäter* – which they earlier translated as 'doer' (GM I: 13). Nietzsche may mean for his readers at this point to recall his earlier discussion of the 'type of human being [who] *needs* to believe in a neutral independent "subject", prompted by an instinct for self-preservation and self-affirmation in which every lie is sanctified' (GM I: 13).
96 See also HH I P6.
97 These three 'innocent' methods – 'the general muting of the feeling of life, mechanical activity, [and] the petty pleasure' (GM III: 19) – may be meant to correspond to the three purposes for which life attempted 'to *exploit* the bad instincts of all sufferers . . . [namely,] self-discipline, self-surveillance and self-overcoming' (GM III: 16).
98 Immediately after claiming that Essay I of GM provides a 'contrast between a *noble* morality and a chandala morality, born of *ressentiment* and impotent vengefulness', Nietzsche identifies Paul as 'the greatest of all apostles of vengeance' (A 45).
99 See A 22.
100 In his review of GM, he boasts that 'this book contains the first psychology of the priest' (EH: gm).

101 See EH: 'destiny' 6.

102 Freud offers a similar and similarly personal reckoning of his own limitations alluding in particular to his 'defensive attitude' toward 'the idea of an instinct of destruction' (p. 67).

103 'Too good' is also how the 'the *majority* of mortals', encouraged by the ascetic ideal, 'attempt to see themselves' vis-à-vis 'this world' (GM III: 1). Nietzsche therefore may mean to signal that he and his fellow psychologists are blinded by their (as yet unacknowledged) allegiance to the ascetic ideal.

104 For an elaboration on this diagnosis, see EH: 'wise' 6.

105 As we have seen, the priestly type is characterized by its internalization of the recriminations directed against it by its community, whose customs and laws the priest knows himself to have abrogated (D 9).

106 See TI 7: 2.

107 This interpretation is supported by his discussion of the 'church' and its efforts to improve 'the noble Teutons' (TI 7: 2).

108 An example of the kind of tale the priest might have told is found at 1 Cor. 1.27–8. See also A 45.

109 See TI 9: 36.

110 In the context of a discussion of Socrates, who also 'seemed to be a physician, a savior', Nietzsche remarks that the 'means' chosen by 'philosophers and moralists' to 'extricat[e] themselves from decadence . . . is but another expression of decadence' (TI 2: 11).

111 See A 7.

112 In the first sentence of the next section, Nietzsche attributes the ruin of 'health and taste' not to the ascetic priest, but to the ascetic ideal (GM III: 23).

113 My interpretation of this section is indebted to Gemes, p. 191.

114 See Loeb.

115 See Gemes, p. 206.

116 For example, his reference to the "Nay-sayers and outsides of today . . ." recalls his description of his "we" in GS 357, which, as we shall see, he actually imports into the text of GM III: 27.

117 He explicitly identifies himself and his "we" as "free spirits" at HH I P7.

118 Kaufmann and Hollingdale offer 'experimentally' to translate the German adverb *versuchsweise*, which is a term of increasing importance in the post-Zarathustran period of Nietzsche's career. A *Versuch* is an *experiment* or an *attempt*, but it also suggests a *temptation* or *enticement*. Nietzsche called his 1886 Preface to the new edition of *The Birth of Tragedy* 'An Attempt at a Self-Criticism' [*Versuch einter Selbstkritik*]. He also suggests *Versucher* as a name for the 'new species of philosopher' that he sees 'coming up' (BGE 42).

119 On 'the self-overcoming [*Selbstüberwindung*] of morality', see EH, 'destiny' 3; and BGE 32.

120 In GS 357 itself, he identifies 'unconditional and honest atheism' as a 'triumph achieved . . . by the European conscience'. He alters this passage for its (unacknowledged) inclusion in GM III: 27.

121 Nietzsche also claims this role for his 'we' in D P4.

122 The self-referential nature of their interrogation of the will to truth may be meant to anticipate, or perhaps facilitate, the 'revaluation of all values', which Nietzsche elsewhere describes as 'an act of supreme self-examination on the part of humankind, become flesh and genius in me' (EH: 'destiny' 1).

123 The wisdom they stand to gain may be related to what Nietzsche elsewhere calls '*tragic wisdom*' (EH: BT 3).

124 He suggests as much in GS 371.

125 Nietzsche's reference to this 'spectacle' [*Schauspiel*] may be meant to recall his earlier reference to the 'Dionysian drama' that has been staged by the 'grand old eternal comic poet of our existence' (GM P: 7).

126 See Loeb.

127 In his review of GM, he identifies his *Zarathustra* as the source of a '*counter-ideal*' (EH: gm).

128 He alludes suggestively to a successor ideal, whose proximity he associates with his capacity for prankish, self-directed mockery, in GM P7; II: 24; III: 3; III: 10. See also GS 382.

129 Here he finally reveals 'what [the ascetic ideal] means; what it indicates; what lies hidden behind it, beneath it, in it; of what it is the provisional, indistinct expression, overlaid with question marks and misunderstandings' (GM III: 23).

130 In a typical expression of this wish, he remarks, 'We sail right *over* morality, we crush, we destroy perhaps the remains of our own morality by daring to make our voyage there – but what matter are *we!*' (BGE 23)

131 See Loeb.

132 See TI 9: 38.

133 See TI 9: 36.

134 Ridley, pp. 150–2.

4. RECEPTION AND INFLUENCE

1 Cited in Hayman, p. 314.

2 Cited in Hayman, p. 314.

3 Hayman, pp. 316–18; Brandes, pp. 82–3.

4 Brandes, p. 63.

5 Brandes, p. 64.

6 Letter to Franz Overbeck on 24 March 1887. SB, Vol. 8, No. 820, p. 48.

7 Brandes, p. 59.

8 Brandes, p. 97.

9 Brandes, p. 104.

10 Nordau, pp. 470–2.

11 Nordau, p. 469.

12 Nordau, p. 451.

13 See Aschheim, pp. 161–3.

14 Aschheim, pp. 249–51.
15 Safranski, pp. 317–18, see also MacIntyre, p. 149–58.
16 Freud, pp. 70–1.
17 The word translated by Strachey as *civilization* is *Kultur*. In their translation of GM, Kaufmann and Hollingdale typically translate *Cultur* as *culture*.
18 Freud, p. 92.
19 Ricoeur, pp. 32–6.
20 Ricoeur, p. 33.
21 Deleuze and Guattari, p. 190.
22 Deleuze and Guattari, p. 190.

BIBLIOGRAPHY

Acampora, C. D. (2006) 'On sovereignty and overhumanity: why it matters how we read Nietzsche's *Genealogy* II: 2', in *Nietzsche's* On the Genealogy of Morals: *Critical Essays*, ed. Christa Davis Acampora. Lanham, MD: Rowman & Littlefield, pp. 147–62.

Aschheim, S. E. (1992) *The Nietzsche Legacy in Germany 1890–1990*. Berkeley: University of California Press.

Ansell Pearson, K. (1997) *Viroid Life: Perspectives on Nietzsche and the Transhuman Condition*. London: Routledge.

Brandes, G. (1914) *Friedrich Nietzsche*, trans. A. G. Chater. London: William Heinemann.

Deleuze, G. and Guattari, F. (1983) *Anti-Oedipus: Capitalism and Schizophrenia*, trans. Robert Hurley, Mark Seem and Helen R. Lane. Minneapolis: University of Minnesota Press.

Freud, S. (1961) *Civilization and Its Discontents*, trans. James Strachey. New York: W. W. Norton & Co.

Gemes, K. (2006) ' "We remain of necessity strangers to ourselves": the key message of Nietzsche's *Genealogy*', in *Nietzsche's* On the Genealogy of Morals: *Critical Essays*, ed. Christa Davis Acampora. Lanham, MD: Rowman & Littlefield, pp. 191–208.

Hatab, L. (1997) *A Nietzschean Defense of Democracy*. Chicago: Open Court.

Hayman, R. (1982) *Nietzsche: A Critical Life*. New York: Penguin Books.

Janaway, C. (2007) *Beyond Selflessness: Reading Nietzsche's* Genealogy. Oxford: Oxford University Press.

Leiter, B. (2001) *Nietzsche on Morality*. London: Routledge.

Loeb, P. S. (2007) 'Suicide, meaning, and redemption', in *Nietzsche on Time and History*, ed. Manuel Dries. Berlin: Walter de Gruyter.

MacIntyre, B. (1992) *Forgotten Fatherland: The Search for Elisabeth Nietzsche*. New York: Farrar Straus Giroux.

Migotti, M. (2006) 'Slave morality, Socrates, and the Bushmen: a critical introduction to *On the Genealogy of Morality, Essay I*', in *Nietzsche's* On the Genealogy of Morals: *Critical Essays*, ed. Christa Davis Acampora. Lanham, MD: Rowman & Littlefield, pp. 109–30.

Nietzsche, F. (1980) *Sämtliche Werke: Kritische Studienausgabe in 15 Bänden*, ed. G. Colli and M. Montinari. Berlin: dtv/de Gruyter.

—— (1986) *Sämtliche Briefe: Kritische Studienausgabe in 8 Bänden*, ed. G. Colli and M. Montinari. Berlin: dtv/de Gruyter.

—— (1996) *On the Genealogy of Morals*, trans. Douglas Smith. Oxford: Oxford University Press.

—— (1998) *On the Genealogy of Morality*, trans. Maudemarie Clark and Alan J. Swensen. Indianapolis: Hackett.

—— (2006) *On the Genealogy of Morality*, trans. Carol Diethe, ed. Keith Ansell Pearson. Cambridge: Cambridge University Press.

Nordau, M. (1993) *Degeneration*, trans. unattributed. Lincoln, NE: University of Nebraska Press.

Orkin, J.D. (2005) 'Nietzsche's Greatest Handicap: A Comparative Analysis of Zahavi's Handicap Principle and *On the Genealogy of Morals*'. Unpublished seminar paper, Pennsylvania State University, University Park, PA.

Owen, D. (2007) *Nietzsche's Genealogy of Morality*. Stocksfield: Acumen Publishing.

Pippin, R.B. (2006) "Lightning and Flash, Agent and Deed (*GM* I:6–17)," in *Nietzsche's* On the Genealogy of Morals: *Critical Essays*, ed. Christa Davis Acampora. Lanham, MD: Rowman & Littlefield, pp. 131–145.

Richardson, J. (2004) *Nietzsche's New Darwinism*. Oxford: Oxford University Press.

Ricoeur, P. (1970) *Freud and Philosophy: An Essay on Interpretation*, trans. Denis Savage. New Haven: Yale University Press.

Ridley, A. (1998) *Nietzsche's Conscience: Six Character Studies from the Genealogy*. Ithaca, NY: Cornell University Press.

Risse, M. (2001) 'The Second Treatise in *On the Genealogy of Morality*: Nietzsche on the origin of the bad conscience', in *European Journal of Philosophy* 9:1, 55–81.

Safranski, R. (2002) *Nietzsche: A Philosophical Biography*, trans. Shelley Frisch. New York: W. W. Norton.

Spencer, H. (1866) *The Principles of Biology, Volume I*. New York: D. Appleton and Co.

Thatcher, D. S. (1989) '*Zur Genealogie der Moral*: some textual annotations', *Nietzsche-Studien* 18, 587–99.

White, R. (1997) *Nietzsche and the Problem of Sovereignty*. Champaign, IL: University of Illinois Press.

Wilcox, J. T. (1997) 'What aphorism does Nietzsche explicate in *Genealogy of Morals*, Essay III?' in *Journal of the History of Philosophy* XXXV/4, 593–610.

Yovel, Y. (1998) *Dark Riddle: Hegel, Nietzsche, and the Jews*. University Park, PA: Penn State Press.

Zahavi, A. and Zahavi, A. (1997) *The Handicap Principle: A Missing Piece of Darwin's Puzzle*. Oxford: Oxford University Press.

INDEX